Aachen Equestrian Beauty

Horse Show to the World

Aachen Equestrian Beauty

Horse Show to the World

John Minoprio

UNICORN

Dedication

This book is dedicated to
Frank Kemperman

CHIO Aachen Show Director 1993–2022

with admiration and grateful thanks

Contents

Foreword

It is the atmosphere that makes the CHIO Aachen
so unique. There is something in the air during the
ten days of the show, an excitement, a shimmering,
a huge joy. Athletes and visitors alike are euphoric,
just so delighted to be there and to become part of
this fabulous experience.

Aachen is a legend, the very heart and soul of equestrian
sport. For many decades the photographer John Minoprio
has captured this unique atmosphere, this Aachen myth,
and so has helped to write the Aachen story himself.

    For me, Aachen is a home game; just one hour away
from my home, coming to Aachen is like coming home. With
John's book, the Aachen feeling is now alive all year round.

Isabell Werth

CHIO prize money is funded by many generous sponsors, both corporate and private individuals. Here is one of the most famous, Rolex, whose total endowment for the Grand Prix of Aachen is €1M. Here is the 2019 winner, Kent Farrington of the United States on Gazelle being presented with his prize by Rafael Rolli, Managing Director Rolex Germany.

Introduction

'The Grand Prix at Aachen… der grosste Preis der Welt'. Words usually spoken in awe, certainly in hushed tones, for the winner has reached the top. The sport is show jumping. My first visit was 1998, the 100th Anniversary of CHIO Aachen. The other 'grosste Preis' was for dressage.

This world famous horse show combines beauty and elegance with impeccable standards. It seems to share with its golfing counterpart, The Masters at Augusta National, a feeling of local tradition combined with an old world sense of good manners, fair play, excellence in all its forms and a knowledgable crowd. This is a grand event in which the citizens of its ancient city take pride. It is a glorious tribute to the horses, who are its stars, and to the fearless competitors, whose feats we gaze at in wonder.

There are a lot of horses. How much we owe them for their generous spirit. CHIO Aachen now includes Eventing, Carriage Driving and Vaulting. An army of owners, trainers, grooms, doctors, vets, physiotherapists, farriers and stable staff, devote themselves to horse and rider success.

The administrative staff assistants, in their stylish Aachen dress, are equally impressive. They take care of VIPs and sponsors, judges, timing, scorers, stewards and competitors, host prize giving, look after exhibitors, cope with thousands of spectators in the stadiums, and deal with the press, commentary systems, catering, arena course building, lighting, maintenance, security and first aid.

With my camera, I tried to record this unique celebration enjoyed by so many – its splendid settings, its wide range of competition, its brilliant horses and riders, its dedicated management and staff, its loyal sponsors, its beauty. The book provides a glimpse into this equestrian wonderland where I spent so many happy hours.

As a boy, on leaving a party, I was taught to say 'thank you.' To everyone at CHIO Aachen, Horse Show to the World, I say 'It was lovely – thank you for having me.'

John Minoprio

The grass in the main stadium is a thing of beauty.
Sometimes it rains in torrents, but this green sward
recovers quickly. Less is more … there is grandeur in
the scale of the arena as it is prepared for the first day.

CHIO supports charities, many concerning the welfare of children. President Carl Meulenbergh said "Over the past years we have been able to pass over a large sum of donations made by generous CHIO visitors." Here, in 2014, a cheque for €60,050 draws media interest and a knowing look.

Rolex unites the four 'majors' of Show Jumping in a prize to dream about. CHIO Aachen, Spruce Meadows, CHI Geneva and The Dutch Masters in s'-Hertogenbosch are the shows. Three wins and the rider receives a bonus of €1M, four wins and it is €2M, while if you win two in direct succession, you pick up a bonus of €500,000. As the song goes, 'Nice Work if you Can Get it.'

Swiss team members parade in style thanks to the loyal and lavish sponsorship of Mercedes-Benz, a company associated with CHIO for nearly 70 years. Mercedes-Benz generosity extends to a chauffeuring service of shuttle vehicles. 'Exclusive' is certainly the word for this fine example of the motor manufacturer's craft. Elitist yes, but why not? This is CHIO and only the best will do.

The highlight is the Nations' Cup. Eight teams
competed over two rounds and there was joy before
the prize giving when Germany won in 2019. The
President of the Aachen-Laurensberger Rennverein e.V.,
Carl Meulenbergh, holds the bouquet. In the centre
is the National Coach, Otto Becker, while Dr Carsten
Oder, Chairman Mercedes-Benz Cars Sales Germany, is
ready with commemorative silver for the winning team.

Dressage is the focus of Deutsche Bank, a sponsor since 1955 and famous for its Deutsche Bank Stadium, home to the greatest riders in the world since 1999. The stately column backdrop had to give way to demand, a gleaming roof was added which increased the crowd capacity to 6300 and turned the stadium into a modern classic. The surrounding practice arenas are a bonus for spectators who can watch the stars ride in, smoothing out any difficulties before their name is called. Ingrid Klimke is preparing to enter the arena.

The Dutch champion, the black stallion Totilas, the wonder horse of world dressage ridden by Edward Gal, brought his own pop festival aura with him whenever he appeared. There was huge interest when he was sold in 2011 to be ridden by Alexander Matthias Rath for Germany. Here, photographers crowd together to take his picture. There are 600 media at CHIO Aachen securing its position as a world sporting event.

It is a rare privilege to enter the stables. They are an oasis of calm, carefully shielded from the public. There is an atmosphere of well ordered serenity. Happy horses here. They must go from their quiet stable sanctuary, perhaps into the huge main stadium with its cheering crowd, but that is their job and they know it.

Opening Ceremony

CHIO enjoys close ties with its 'Partner Country' which assumes the role of Guest of Honour. Examples are Switzerland, Italy, The Netherlands, France and China. The Partner Country stages lavish displays.

Children join in the traditional
Opening Ceremony flag waving
and march proudly into the
40,000 capacity Main Stadium.

An immaculate quadrille
of The Royal Netherlands
Mounted Brigade.

Cavalry school precision marks the entry of members of the Aachener Stadtreiter who have special stewarding duties at the show. These include taking charge of the Rolex Grand Prix Trophy and escorting prizewinners in the stadium.

On parade is the Cadre Noir, a corps of écuyers or instructors at the French Military Riding Academy in Saumur. Its name comes from the black uniforms and it is one of the most prestigious classical riding academies in the world.

In 2011 the Partner Country was Italy. A parade
of flag bearing Vespa scooters, the mounted
Carabinieri in their magnificent Gala uniforms.

Switzerland, Partner Country
in 2014, provided a display by
the Berner Dragoner, the 18th
century parade troop and Guards
of Honour of the State of Bern.

Partner Country. The
Netherlands – lady riders
in swallowtail orange,
a smiling beauty in the
tricolour of red white
and blue, and a sparkling
ambassador on behalf of
Dutch cheese.

China prefers history. Mounted archery, the ability to shoot while riding a horse, has long been a tradition of Chinese warfare. Skill with the bow, a weapon founded 4000 years ago, was encouraged and expected. The Partner Country of 2018 echoes its Terracotta Army while manpower enables the Chinese dragon to enter the stadium.

The explosion of young talent in the 1960s led Diana Vreeland, editor of *Vogue*, to refer to it as 'youthquake'. At CHIO, youth is to the fore. In 2022 Aachen hosted the FEI Youth Equestrian Games. Many young riders have the thrill of showing in the main stadium and here are some enjoying themselves.

"I wish I had painted more women riding side-saddle before the fashion died out. A good figure and a well-cut habit is the essence of grace and symmetry."

– Sir Alfred Munnings

Munnings would be glad to see the fashion has not quite died out. Here the Side-Saddle Association prepares to enter the main stadium for its display, while Amy Bryan-Dowell on her trusted grey hunter shows the way.

Dressage

In 1960, CHIO Aachen held a significant event, the 24th International Dressage Jumping and Driving Tournament, first held in 1927. Watched by 175,000 spectators, this competition stamped CHIO Aachen with the hallmark of excellence, thus beginning its rise to world renown.

Germany dominated. In show jumping Alwyn Schockemohle won the Prize of Europe while in dressage, Harry Boldt drew the crowds. Although dressage was founded by the Ancient Greeks, as a spectator sport it was new. CHIO Aachen hosted the first European Dressage Championship in 1967 when Dr Reiner Klimke became Champion of Europe. CHIO endorsed its support for dressage when the superb Deutsche Bank Stadium, seating 6300 people, was built in 2014.

    The Aachen Dressage Grand Prix winners bear the stamp of greatness – Boldt, Neckermann, Klimke, Stuckelberger, Theodoruscu, Capellmann, van Grunsven, Gal, Dujardin ... and most honoured of all, Isabell Werth.

In his autobiography, Colonel Alois Podhajsky of The Spanish Riding School writes: "I myself once asked an American why the applause broke out in the quadrille at the change from the walk to the gallop. Something we had not met before. His prompt answer impressed me particularly as a rider: 'Well, it is hard enough to strike off at canter from a walk with one horse, but to have eight horses doing this at the same time without the slightest raggedness is to my mind a work of art.'"

Yes, especially at CHIO Aachen, dressage is a work of art and a thing of beauty.

Monica Theodorescu is a three times Olympic Medallist, World Champion and double European champion with the team, winner of the Deutsche Bank Prize, the Grand Prix of Aachen. In 2012, she was the first woman to be appointed National Trainer to the German team. Here she rides Whisper in the Havens Pferdefutter Prize in 2007.

The late Duke and Duchess of Richmond were generous benefactors of dressage in England. The Championships they held for 20 years in the grounds of historic Goodwood House, built in 1600, had a charm all of their own. It meant the world's best came to Goodwood. There, I first saw Harry Boldt, Reiner Klimke and Christine Stuckelberger, and joined in a mighty cheer for Jennie Loriston – Clarke when she won bronze in the World Championships in 1978. British dressage owes much to the Duke and Duchess of Richmond.

But another rider caught my eye, Dominique d'Esmé. She was remarkably effective, steady and calm, down in the saddle, completely at one with the horse. Not surprising. She competed for France in 5 Olympic Games. It was good to see her again at CHIO in 2007 on Roi de Coeur, the horse she had ridden at top level for so many years.

One of the early British riders who decided to train on the Continent of Europe with considerable success was Emma Hindle. She began in Sweden and then moved to Germany. She rode her horse Lancet in the Beijing Olympics and finished 7th as well as competing in the Athens Olympics. She rode Chequille at Aachen in 2007.

Emma quotes her sporting philosophy as: "There is no perfect dressage horse. I like them to be active and to have good self-carriage, three good paces, and be willing to work."

Inessa Merkulova of Russia riding in. The year is 1998. "Everything was beautiful at the Ballet", a song from A Chorus Line, seems right. Dressage is equestrian dance. Did not Colonel Alois Podhajsky, director of the Spanish Riding School Vienna, call his autobiography My Dancing White Horses?

Anky van Grunsven, the soon to be famous Dutch rider as Dressage Olympic Champion supreme, rides in at CHIO in 1998. Her triple Individual Gold would inspire a generation.

Dutch rider Coby van Baalen in 1998. She was in the Netherlands team in the Sydney Olympics 2000. She won Team Silver and came fifth. She describes coming second to Anky van Grunsven in CHIO Rotterdam on Ferro in 1998 as 'her most beautiful memory'. Immensely experienced, she runs a dressage stable and breeding establishment with her daughter Marlies and son Arie Jr. Her Coby Van Baalen Foundation supports para dressage.

In the Aachen stadium for the prize giving, Coby is followed by the Finnish dressage rider and famous trainer Kyra Kyrkland who has competed in six Olympic Games.

In her mother's shoes. Coby's daughter Marlies rides her test on BMC Phoebe DVB against the stately architectural background of the Aachen dressage arena in 2011.

In 2008 Adelinde Cornelissen, brought up on a farm, left her job as an English teacher in the Netherlands for a career as a dressage rider. To judge from her medal tally in world dressage, this was a good move. With her chestnut Jerich Parzival, which she had for 21 years, she distilled dressage delight, receiving the Best Athlete Award from the International Equestrian Federation (FEI) in 2011 and an Individual Olympic Silver in 2012.

Hans Peter Minderhoud on Zanardi in 2018. The Dutch rider won the World Championship for 5-year-old horses in 2004, and the 6-year-old title the following year. He has won Team Gold Medals at the World Championships at Kentucky and the European Championships in 2007 and in 2015 at Aachen. In 2016 he won the Gold Medal in the FEI World Cup Final riding Glock's Dream Boy. He has competed in three Olympic Games.

Fabienne Müller-Lütkemeier was a member of the Gold Medal winning German team at the 2013 European Dressage Championships riding D'Agostino. She is the niece of Nadine Capellmann, 2002 Dressage World Champion and twice winner of the Grand Prix of Aachen.

Steffen Peters on his famous horse Ravel, 4th in the Dressage Championship in 2011. They won The Grand Prix Dressage of Aachen in 2009. A veteran of five Olympic Games, with two Bronze Team medals and one Silver to his name, Steffen was born in Wesel, but emigrated to America in 1984. He became a US citizen in 1992 and is a holder of many US Equestrian Federation honours. His medal haul grows with his horse Suppenkasper.

It seems that dressage riders with an eye on the Gold Medal spot start young, say aged four or five. Jessica von Bredow-Werndel was no exception. She persevered, together with her brother Ben, helped by a succession of trainers and stars, including Isabell Werth. Her decisive win, both Team and Individual Gold at the Tokyo Olympics, riding TSF Dalera Bb, proved her talent and her love of young horses, training them, improving them and enjoying what they give her back in return. She stresses concentration … 'It is always work and training to have everything together here and now.'

Preparation and attention to detail counts. The practice arenas for dressage are well placed next to the stables. 'The more I work and practice, the luckier I seem to get,' said the Grand Slam golfer Gary Player.

Kristina Bröring-Sprehe won many medals with her Hanoverian stallion Desperados, including team and Grand Prix Special bronze and Kur Silver at the 2015 European Championships at Aachen. A year later they won the Grand Prix of Aachen, and that's the top, ranking surely with an Oscar in Hollywood. Here she competes on Desperados in 2014. Kristina was shattered when the horse died suddenly aged 19. She wrote: "You made me … you will always be my heart horse."

There was surprise in 2011 when Alexander Matthias Rath appeared riding the champion dressage stallion Totilas for Germany. What had become of his Dutch rider Edward Gal who rode him last year to win the Grand Prix of Aachen?

German buyers, scenting victory in the London Olympics to come, had bought Totilas for an undisclosed sum, believed to be "an offer you can't refuse." Here is Alexander Matthias Rath riding Totilas at Aachen in 2011. He had to take over and ride a sensitive horse, but he was still good enough to win the Grand Prix.

Lisa Wilcox came from a non-horsey family of seven, but was determined to go her own way and make her name in the world of dressage. She worked in Germany, notably with Ernst Hoyos, a former trainer at the Spanish Riding School, whom she credits with expanding her knowledge and developing her riding skills.

She returned to the United States and was chosen for the 2004 Olympics with her horse Relevant when she won a team bronze medal.

How do actors become so good? Laurence Olivier watched people, how they moved, their gestures, the way they walked. One who watched horses was Katherine Bateson-Chandler.

She was groom to the famous American Olympic dressage rider, and later team trainer, Robert Dover. She was 17 years with Dover who insisted from the start she watch him ride his horses and judge his performance. Katherine developed what photographers call 'the seeing eye.'

Urged by Robert Dover to launch out on her own, super groom Katherine, who watched from the ground, rose to the top on her horse Alcazar. Here she is leaving the arena on Alcazar in 2019.

In a video clip, US multiple medallist Adrienne Lyle, said what she loved most about her horses was that "Every day when you work with them, you learn something not only about them, but about yourself." That surely is the right attitude for a sympathetic competitor and perhaps an extension of what my late father-in-law always said: "Horses are good for the character."

Adrienne Lyle was voted the US International Equestrian Athlete of the Year 2022. Here she rides Harmony's Duval at Aachen in 2019.

Brought up on a farm in Vermont, Laura Graves persuaded her parents to trade what were once known as 'consumer durables' to allow the family to keep two ponies. Keen to go further, Laura and her mother bought a foal from the Netherlands, but the young horse proved tricky, throwing Laura and breaking her back. So she decided to sell the horse and study cosmetology, but his wayward character meant there were no takers. His name was Verdades. Laura resolved to try again as a dressage rider.

In a feat of courage and perseverance, she reached Grand Prix level and qualified for the 2014 World Equestrian Games. She made the US team and has won many medals. A fine example of "If at first you don't succeed, try again."

Jill de Ridder was a member of the gold medal winning German team that competed at the 2007 and 2010 European Junior Riders Championships. Here, riding Whitney, she is on her home ground, and hallowed ground it is, for she comes from Aachen.

Long ago, when things were not quite as they are now, gentlemen, while welcoming the appearance of ladies in the hunting field, would make way for a horse ridden by 'a slip of a girl.'

Today even 'girl' is frowned on. But, when you see Victoria Max-Theurer riding powerful dressage horses you know what they meant. She has competed for Austria in 5 Olympic Games and 9 European Championships. As the daughter of Elisabeth Theurer, the 1980 Individual Dressage Olympic Champion, she was born to ride horses.

Carl Hester has played a key role in the success of dressage in England. Young riders have been inspired by his winning talent as an Olympic rider and trainer. From the age of four he was brought up in the tiny Channel Island of Sark, where he rode a donkey on the steep paths. No saddle. "You need to ride without a saddle giving you core strength … that's when I learned about balance."

That generous benefactor of British dressage, the late Dr Wilfried Bechtolsheimer, or 'Doctor B', as he was known, spotted Carl's talent and gave him horses to ride, including his own stallion Giorgione, on which he competed in the 1992 Barcelona Olympics.

Carl, in an act of selfless goodwill, followed Dr B's example. He gave his horse Valegro to his assistant trainer Charlotte Dujardin and set her on a path to two Olympic Gold Medals, not forgetting the 2014 Grand Prix of Aachen.

Charlotte Dujardin on her own horse Fernandez in 2011, her first appearance at CHIO. How could we guess that this unknown girl from England would break dressage records? What were the odds on her becoming European Champion, Olympic Champion and World Champion, her honours thick upon her?

She discarded her top hat in favour of the latest from a company who started making motor cycle helmets in 1911. Perhaps this was a good omen for, on Valegro, she reached the heights.

In 2019, a youthful slim rider on a powerful black horse appeared. She would go far. Charlotte Fry, known as Lottie, had a distinctive saddle cloth proclaiming her link with Anne Van Olst, the vastly experienced Danish rider, trainer and breeder. The power and beauty of a dressage stallion shows as Lottie rides Everdale in 2022. She came 7th in the Grand Prix with the last six places separated by a mere 1.23 marks.

Lottie began her competitive career aged 10 trained by her mother Laura, an Olympic rider who died of cancer at the age of 45. In a Horse & Hound interview, Lottie said of her mother: "The thing that influenced me the most about her was her work ethic. She worked so hard for what she did and she loved the horses so much … that's really rubbed off on me, I think."

In 2022, Lottie won the World Dressage Championship.

In 2004, the English banned foxhunting, but they discovered something else, dressage.

When dressage was awakening in England, Laura Bechtolsheimer (now Mrs Mark Tomlinson) was one of the heroes. The daughter of Dr Wilfried Bechtolsheimer, a remarkable benefactor of British dressage, she arrived in England from Germany aged one. At thirteen she decided to concentrate on dressage and fast tracked to the top. From 2004 to 2012, with her magnificent chestnut Mistral Hojris, she was reliably present in the prize-giving line up. She competed at Aachen and showed her class when placed third in the Grand Prix Championship in 2011.

Success led to the Olympic Games 2012 when she won a Team Gold Medal and an Individual Bronze. The honours did not stop there, for services to dressage Laura was made a Member of the Order of The British Empire.

Kristy Oatley of Australia rides Quando-Quando in 2007. Born in Sydney she has represented Australia in four Olympic Games.

You could not miss two young riders in Spanish colours. They were Juan Matute Guimon and his sister Paula. Son and daughter of Juan Guimon, who competed in three Olympic Games, Juan Jr is an Olympic rider who looks the part in every way, at least the girls of Aachen seemed to think so. He has the looks of a bullfighter to rival Luis Miguel Dominguin. He rides Don Diego Ymas.

A near fatal illness in 2020 shocked the dressage world, but he fought his way back into the saddle and is trained by his father in Wellington, Florida. May his courage be rewarded.

His sister Paula rides Tarpan Ymas at CHIO in 2014. She has her own business PMG Stables, based in Wellington. Her maxim is: "I believe we are all placed on this earth with a mission. Mine is to bring people closer to horses."

Morgan Barbançon Mestre rode for Spain aged 20 in the London Olympics 2012. With Spanish/French parentage she now represents France. Here in 2015 she rides in against the white background loved by catalogue photographers. She looks up and straight ahead. The tendency of dressage riders to look down may be necessary when schooling, but in the arena dressage is a performance requiring stage presence.

There are 1000 horses at CHIO, but you do have favourites. Fuego XII is one, ridden here by Juan Manuel Munoz Diaz. He is what the auctioneer at a horse sale in Holland would describe as 'super nice'. Those who saw his sensational Grand Prix Kur performance in the 2010 World Equestrian Games in Kentucky would agree. His rider said of him "During competition he always felt very important and proud ..." He is a Pure Spanish Horse (PRE) and as he leaves the arena, even in a quiet walk, you feel his grandeur, his composure, his sense of occasion.

Spain's Claudio Castilla Ruiz is quoted as saying "Sport is demanding and tough, but I try never to lose my smile." A most endearing aim. The smile in professional sport can become more of a snarl. Dressage is so precise and requires such concentration and poise that the smile for the judges after the final salute lights up the arena. Horse and rider can relax after their intense effort. The relief is plain to see and the wave to supporters joyful.

Judy Reynolds on Vancouver K in 2019. As a young rider, she was a pathfinder for dressage in Ireland. At 21, she was at the top and ambitiously seeking stronger competition outside Ireland. She decide to go to Germany where she worked with a number of trainers before establishing her business. She is a thoroughgoing dressage professional who represented Ireland at the Rio de Janeiro Olympics of 2016.

Judy Reynolds is a dedicated trainer who delights in bringing on horses and teaching the young. She continues to work in Ireland. Her desire to see dressage flourish in her home country remains. She has done much to make it happen, passing on her undoubted skills, learned in her own long Continental apprenticeship.

The three times Danish Champion and Olympic Team Bronze Medallist in Beijing, Anne Van Olst, is a remarkable contributor to dressage in Denmark, not only as a rider, but in her later career as a breeder and trainer through Van Olst Horses. She has competed in the Olympic Games five times. Anne proved her maxim "Strive for the highest achievable quality in everything" when a Van Olst stallion, ridden by her pupil Charlotte Fry, won the World Championship in 2022. Here she rides Exquis Clearwater in 2011.

A triumph for Denmark's Cathrine Dufour and Vamos Amigos, a bay stallion, owned by Sarah Pidgeley, as she beat the best to win the Aachen Grand Prix in 2022. A common feature in the rise of dressage champions is that they start young (in this case aged 5) devotedly supported by parents who are not horsey, but recognise talent. They find a trainer to inspire and away they go.

Cathrine was no exception. Her climb to the top came via the Rio and Tokyo Olympics and her name on the Grand Prix winners board at Aachen ensures her place in history. Yet, she still has much to play for. Her success renewed interest in dressage in Denmark. Here she rides Bohemian.

The support teams of today are large. They not only include owners, sponsors, trainers and grooms, but there is a wealth of 'subject matter experts' to be called upon. Vets, farriers, saddlers, physiotherapists, sports psychologists, arrangers of music and gymnasts are engaged in pursuit of medal glory.

Differing reactions as the German Dressage team and their connections gather at the European Championships at CHIO Aachen in 2015. Left to right: rider Jessica von Bredow-Werndl, coach Jonny Hilberath, owner Madeleine Winter-Schulze, trainer Monica Theodorescu, Chef d'Equipe Klaus Roeser, and rider Alexander Matthias Rath.

Support

A distinguished Chairman of Selectors, in this case the game was cricket, said: "When in doubt go for class." Madeleine Winter-Schulze, through her generous support, made sure her horses bore the hallmark of class. She loves horses. Her riders are her close family and the most famous are Ludger Beerbaum and Isabell Werth.

The Sunshine of Your Smile could be Madeleine's signature song. You don't have to photograph her to know she is a lady of great warmth and kindness. She is always smiling, as if to say "I'm having a great time."

Madeleine is seen here with Isabell Werth after winning the 2018 Aachen Grand Prix with Emilio. Their brilliant partnership has led to many victories. Madeleine's financial backing for riders is a matter of wonder. It has brought success and joy to so many. Thank you, Ma'am.

A rapturous Ann-Kathrin Linsenhoff, a 1988 Olympic Team Gold Medallist, after Totilas won the Grand Prix. She bought the horse in partnership with Paul Schockemöhle, the show jumping star and dealer, seen with microphone. An eager press asked for the story, but the Olympic dream ended sadly. Alexander Matthias Rath became ill and was forced to withdraw from the London Games.

Wild rumours spread when news came that German buyers had acquired the dressage wonder horse Totilas, ridden for the Netherlands by Edward Gal, for an astronomic price with the London Olympics in mind. The rider was to be Alexander Matthias Rath, seen here on Totilas, followed by his delighted connections, on his way to receive the Grand Prix of Aachen in 2011.

Jessica von Bredow-Werndl appears aghast, while coach Jonny Hilberath has the look of 'future shock', too much change in too little time. But what have they seen? Or heard?

Afterwards, success is sweet
for Germany's team coach.

Born in Vienna, Ernst Hoyos joined the Spanish Riding School at the age of 18 and spent 29 years there. When your aim is to teach dressage, this grounding must be the perfect preparation. The Spanish Riding School has been teaching classical dressage since 1735. Ernst went to Germany and coached Olympic Team Medallists Ulla Sallzgeber and Lisa Wilcox, glad to draw on his vast experience. Here in 2015, the Polish rider Katarzyna Milczarek listens intently.

'A' stands for Anky. The triple Olympic Gold Medallist Anky van Grunsven helped with the training of the Belgian team ... what a chance for their young riders. Here Anky watches Fanny Verliefden on Annarico working in 2015.

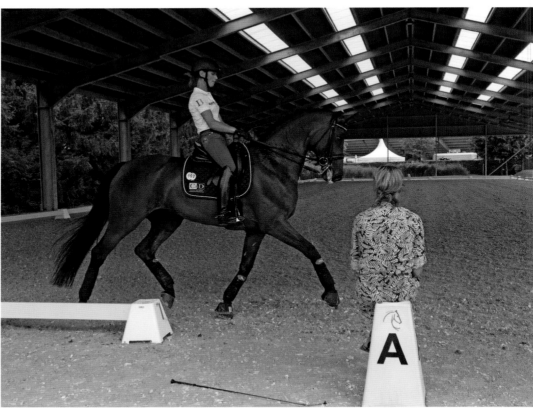

As befits Aachen's
Queen of Dressage, the
champion Isabell Werth
is greeted by a 'high five'
as she leaves the arena.

No list of winners could leave out Anky Van Grunsven. The Dutch rider won Olympic Dressage Individual Gold Medals in Sydney, Athens and Beijing with her horses Bonfire and Salinero – a spectacular achievement. In 2004, riding Salinero, she won the Grand Prix of Aachen and in 2006, the Individual Freestyle Gold Medal at the World Equestrian Games at Aachen.

At the World Equestrian Games in 1994 riding Bonfire her freestyle performance, according to Carl Hester, "changed the world of dressage forever." To honour his memory a statue of Bonfire was erected in Erp, Anky's birthplace.

They should mine and mint a special gold medal for Anky van Grunsven for winning three times running. As they say "she'll go down in history."

Steffen Peters' mount Suppenkasper
stands calm and obliging as his
United States support team members,
including a rider, go to work.

Robert Dover competed for the United States in six Olympic Games and won four Team Bronze Medals. He is an honoured member of the United States Dressage Federation Hall of Fame. Before being appointed coach to the US Dressage team, in 2013 he was appointed Technical Advisor / Chef d'Equipe to the US National Dressage Team. Here he is, having a quiet word, in 2014.

Vet Dr Andre Buthe and groom Alan Smith accompany Carl Hester out of the arena during the European Championships of 2015. The emphasis on animal welfare and the monitoring of the world's best competition horses is assured at CHIO. The well-equipped Veterinary Centre provides professional backup.

Helen Langehanenberg, who won the Grand Prix of Aachen in 2012 and 2013, receives the attention to detail she deserves.

Close support to her rider Natalie Pai en route to the Deutsche Bank stadium. And an air of expectancy. The test takes only a few minutes, yet reputations are at stake.

Grooms behind the scenes at CHIO are easily overlooked amid the glamour of the Aachen arena. We should admire their professionalism and cheer their dedication.

One of the beauties of CHIO is the
sympathetic crowd control. You can walk
freely and perhaps encounter the stars. This
youthful French couple have found theirs.

He looks to have an eye for a horse
and only high performance will do. Has
he come from the heart of America?
There's no doubt of his support.

Mexican wave is described as a wave like movement by the crowd at a sports game. I did not think I would see this at Aachen, but in 2011, there it was.

How was it? New Zealand's Mark Todd tells the story to mixed reactions from his supporters.

Family values. Diederik van Silfhout with his father Alex, a former competitor at World Cup events and coach to the Dutch national dressage team.

Maria Guimon with her daughter Paula. Both dressage rider Paula and her brother Juan Matute Guimon rode for Spain at Aachen.

Show Jumping

The officers of the Cavalry School in Hanover set the standard which made winning at Aachen the cherished goal of every show jumper. President Hindenburg presented the Hindenberg Trophy as "The Nations Cup Prize "in 1933. This prompted thrilling contests between Italy and Germany in the 1930's.

After the war, the duel between the two countries persisted with the emergence of the great show jumpers, Hans Günter Winkler for Germany and the D'Inzeo brothers, Piero and Raimondo, for Italy.

Enter the show jumping arena at CHIO Aachen and Winston Churchill's: "My tastes are simple, I am easily satisfied with the best" comes to mind. And this is the best – the sheer scale, the perfectly placed jumps, the surface with its enviable green sward, the immaculate officials, the roar of the crowd.

Then the riders ... Stand close to the huge fences as their horses soar over, then turn on a sixpence, racing against the clock. Yes, this is the best.

Luciana Diniz of Portugal on Fit For Fun.

John Whitaker
competing at CHIO in
2007. Note the hands,
light and easy, it seems
he could almost be
playing a concert piano.

John Whitaker, at 66, walking the course in 2022.
His long career began with the horse Ryan's Son,
an unlikely candidate for the soaring heights of
show jumping. Ryan's Son looked like a carthorse.
But John started him from scratch and rode him
brilliantly. He was a great crowd pleaser, with his
kick-back buck at the end of every round. Ryan's Son
kick started the Whitaker family as a show jumping
dynasty. John Whitaker competed in 6 Olympic
Games. He won the Grand Prix of Aachen in 1997
and many other titles and is still riding at top level.

John's younger brother Michael also reached the
top, announcing his arrival in glory when he won
the famous Hickstead Derby at the age of 20. An
Olympic rider and winner of numerous prizes he
won the Grand Prix of Aachen in 2012. Here he
rides GIG Amai, his Grand Prix winner, in 2011.

Harry Charles, has the bloodline for the job. He is the son of Team Olympic Gold and European Individual Champion Peter Charles. By Whitaker family standards, at 24, he has a long career ahead. He competed in the Tokyo Olympics, a reminder that Pat Smythe, a famous lady show jumper 70 years ago, called her autobiography Jump for Joy.

One who has made history is the Scottish show jumper, Scott Brash. He is the only winner of the Grand Slam, a phenomenal achievement. Success in four great Horse Shows – CHIO Aachen, Spruce Meadows, CHI Geneva and 's-Hertogenbosch – gains the Grand Slam six figure bonus.

Describing winning the Rolex Grand Slam in 2015 as his most memorable sporting achievement, Scott Brash added: "I believe you can only achieve exceptional things if you build a partnership with a horse and that takes time and trust."

Ben Maher points Explosion W at the fence like an archer aiming an arrow. In 2020 his perfect round won him the Individual Gold medal at the Tokyo Olympic Games. The first British show jumper to be placed No 1 in the world rankings, Ben Maher has competed in four Olympic Games. At 6ft (1.83 m) tall Ben Maher seems an ideal pilot for the big chestnut, a formidable pair, rhythmic, effortless and fast. To prove it, go online to watch their winning round in Tokyo. Majestic.

Meredith Michaels-Beerbaum has had many firsts ... these include being the first woman to ride for Germany in the European Championships and the first female show jumper to reach No 1 in the FEI Rankings. She was born in Los Angeles and competed seriously as a child, Then, while studying at Princeton University, she took a break and switched to riding education with Paul Schockemöhle in Germany.

The Coat of Arms of Germany, the German Eagle, adorns the fence and Ludger Beerbaum, an eagle indeed in the world of show jumping, soars over it. He is a superstar, a multiple World No 1 Ranked Show Jumper, he won four Olympic Gold Medals and was three times winner of the Grand Prix of Aachen. Ludger's father wanted him to have riding lessons aged eight, but he was scared. Then a friend took him to the stables after school. Reassured, he not only took up riding, but found he was good at it.

Meredith Michaels-Beerbaum riding Shutterfly to win the Warsteiner Prize in 2011 before her famous horse retired after an illustrious career. Shutterfly won the Rolex Grand Prix of Aachen in 2005.

Christian Ahlmann on his way to winning his first Rolex Grand Prix of Aachen in 2014. He rides Codex One. His talent was spotted early and at the age of 14 he was one of the youngest riders ever to receive the prized Goldenes Reitabzeichen for proven success. His calm approach has brought him many medals. In 2021 and 2022 he was named Best Rider of the Global Champions League. He says "I still want to sit in the saddle at the age of 70 – simply because riding is fun for me."

Marcus Ehning shows his relief, but coolly retains his calm demeanour, as the last fence, appropriately named Rolex, stays in place after his decisive clear round to win the Grand Prix of Aachen in 2018. Riding Pret A Tout, this was his second Rolex win after his success with Kuhengirl in 2006. To seal his place as one of the all-time greats, Marcus Ehning won a third Rolex Grand Prix on Stargold in 2023. Gold indeed! The prize money has risen to €500,000 for the winner.

There was an exuberant sense of power, a springy will to win, whenever DSP Alice, ridden by Simone Blum, entered her favourite arena, the Main Stadium at Aachen. A member of the winning German Nations Cup team in 2018, the following year Simone and Alice won the Halla Trophy for the most successful horse at CHIO Aachen.

Simone Blum found the mare as a 7-year-old in 2014 and by 2018 they had scaled the heights, winning the World Championship at Tryon, the first lady rider to do so. "I wouldn't be where I am now without Alice" said a grateful Simone.

Jana Wargers on Limbridge for Germany touches down in a rain storm. The weather can quickly change and you are unlucky if you catch it. Jana was a member of the winning Nations Cup team in 2022. She was the first to go, a daunting pressure point for a newcomer. But she had great confidence in Limbridge amid the unique and thrilling atmosphere of the Aachen Main Stadium.

Philipp Weishaupt jumping LB Convall in the Mercedes-Benz Nations Cup in 2017. His two clear rounds helped Germany to victory. In 2016 he won the Rolex Grand Prix of Aachen and the Grand Prix at Spruce Meadows.

Mercedes-Benz Nations Cup Parade. Three famous US riders in 2017 – Laura Kraut, Beezie Madden and McLain Ward.

Legendary film star Gary Cooper, tall in the saddle, began as an extra in Westerns. The nonchalant way he got on a horse singled him out. He was six foot three, the same height as Daniel Deusser, a top box office star in the world of show jumping. A team Olympic bronze medallist in 2016 he won the Rolex Grand Prix of Aachen in 2021.

Deusser, known as Double D, a member of many German teams, has achieved World No 1 ranking. He believes "You can't do it alone". He patiently produces horses with his team. It could be the best is yet to come.

Kent Farrington won the Rolex Grand Prix of Aachen riding
Gazelle in 2019 He is described as 'the Master of Faster'. Brought
up in Chicago, he has made his own way in a career strewn with
international trophies. A compact figure, when so many riders are
tall these days, he is neat in the saddle. Horse and rider appear
moulded together as one. He had victory in his sights in the jump
off for the Rolex Grand Prix of 2014 after a lightning fast round.
But he seems to know that the last fence will fall and the four fault
penalty handed the prize to Christian Ahlmann, slower, but clear.

In the 2008 Beijing Olympics Laura Kraut won a Team Gold Medal for the United States. Her long career stretches back to her first big prize win in 1988. Here she rides Cedric which she describes as her favourite horse of all time.

29-year-old Gerrit Nieberg sprung to fame when, last to go, he grabbed the 2022 Aachen Grand Prix from Scott Brash, the Rolex Grand Slam maestro. But Gerrit's family values are in the right place. His father Lars won two Olympic Gold Medals and he has been brought up with horses.

Here, riding Ben 431, he enjoys his lap of honour. He acknowledges his family, a real team, has been hugely helpful in his career.

Beezie Madden is another long time show jumping legend. Born in Wisconsin she applied the American dream to show jumping. She became the first woman to earn $1M in prize money from the sport. She was the first rider to win the USEF Equestrian of the Year title five times. Here she stretches Coral Reef Via Volo over the water in the 2011 Rolex Grand Prix.

Margie Engel was born in Wellington Florida and at 64
has had the talent to keep going at the top level. She won
6 World Cups and 20 Nations Cups between 1984 and
2005 and competed in the Sydney Olympics in 2000. In
1987 she recorded a then world record high jump of 7 ft
8¾ in. Margie, by the way, is 5 ft 1 in. She is relentlessly
brave, having had many unlucky injuries over the years.
In 2021, she was admitted to the US Show Jumping Hall
of Fame. She is seen in 2014 riding her powerful 16.2 hh
Oldenburg stallion, Royce. What a career, what a star.

Reed Kessler, United States, riding Cylana in 2014. A tight turn, 1/1,000 second, and she was gone. She remains a picture of composure at speed. She is supremely fit. She works out and that includes boxing training where she's fast with both hands. At 18, she qualified for the 2012 London Olympics, the youngest show jumper ever to take part.

Like many CHIO Aachen stars, McLain Ward started young. Encouraged by parents in the horse business, he repaid them when, aged 14, he won the United States Equestrian Federation's Show Jumping Derby, the youngest rider to do so. He followed that by becoming the youngest ever rider to earn $1M in prize money from grand prix competition. Five times an Olympic medallist, the photographs show his style, his calm mastery, his balance and strength in a galloping turn.

Vive La France! French riders taking part in the Mercedes-Benz parade.

Penelope Leprevost on the grey stallion Mylord Carthago in 2014, a picture of professional cool. She won a team Gold Medal at the 2016 Rio Olympic Games. She lives up to the title of her autobiography Destinee Cavaliere. And she is a 'Pony Club Paperback Writer' with her series of Penny children's books for young riders.

Here she is stretching over the Mercedes-Benz fence on Flora de Mariposa, her Olympic horse, in the European Championships of 2015.

Gregory Wathelet of Belgium, riding Conrad de Hus, has just missed the Individual Gold Medal in the European Championships in 2015. An Olympic Team Bronze Medallist and Aachen Grand Prix winner, Gregory Wathelet astonished onlookers in Paris when Conrad lost his bridle three fences out. The pair calmly completed a clear round. He was the flag bearer for Belgium in the Tokyo Olympics Closing Ceremony.

McLain Ward. Asked for his 10 tips for show jumping success, number one was 'Always think of your position' and 'it begins with your head. As a show jumper there is nothing more important than a great overview. You need to keep your eyes up constantly …'. Here he is, 'eyes up'.

Henrik von Eckermann of Sweden is an admirer of Ludger Beerbaum and Madeleine Winter-Schulze. Their work together in show jumping has inspired him. On his chestnut horse King Edward he has been the man to beat, winning the World Cup Final in Omaha in 2023.

The Nations Cup on the Thursday evening. Floodlights on, umbrellas up, as the rain pours down. But look at the total focus of Visconti du Telman, the mount of France's Kevin Staut. Unperturbed, he soars over the fence in copybook style.

Staut has three Olympic medals, individual silver, team bronze and team gold. He has been European Champion four times and is an ambassador for the French Equestrian Federation. Beginning with his individual gold medal in the French Junior Championship in 1995 aged 15 he has had a gilt edged career.

Olivier Robert representing France in the Nations Cup in 2019. He rides the grey stallion Vangog du Mas Garnier to help France to third place. A talented footballer, he had to choose and settled for show jumping. In 2018 he won the French Championships at Fontainebleau.

Another Swiss rider of eminence, Martin Fuchs first rode at CHIO in the European Championships in 2015 at the age of 23, since then he has won the World Cup and the European Championship and been ranked No 1 in the world. Here he rides Leone Jei.

Steve Guerdat of Switzerland competing in the Mercedes-Benz Nations Cup in 2014 riding Nasa. The rider seems to be giving everything to his horse, who shows utter contentment. Only the knees touch the saddle and the hands are feather light. But Steve Guerdat is a man apart, the winner of an Individual Olympic Gold Medal for Show Jumping in London, he was the first rider to win an Individual Olympic Gold medal for Switzerland since 1924. He has won three World Cups and is the current European Champion. He is a dedicated professional with a record to prove it.

Lucy Davis riding Barron won a Team Silver for the USA in the 2016 Olympic Games in Rio. Here, in 2014, she rides Cassis 54.

Fit For Fun 13 ridden by Luciana Diniz in the Rolex Grand Prix in 2017. Cheered on by Luciana's enthusiastic supporters, Fit for Fun jumped her heart out but missed the prize by a second.

Luciana points to the mare as if to say: "She's the bright star, I owe it all to her." And there was something owing ... her prize for second place was €200,000. The following year, 2018, Fit For Fun was second again, with a double clear.

Ursula von der Leyen, President of the European Commission greets Luciana warmly and is one of the first to congratulate her.

If you were born in Dublin, you might consider winning the Aga Khan Trophy for Ireland four times, with the President watching, as your greatest achievement, but Cian O'Connor has done much besides. He has competed at three Olympic Games, four World championships and six European Championships. He is a successful coach to young riders and is known for his eye for a horse. The photograph could double as an advertisement for the Irish horse. The grey mare Irenice Horta in 2019, cleared for take off, undercarriage retracted, shows equine aerodynamics at their finest.

Darragh Kenny on
Imothep in the Nations
Cup 2014. He has
represented Ireland at the
top level for many years.

When you consider the weight of a horse could be half a ton (500kg) and a horse's legs are slender, good landings are desirable. The heights jumped in the Main Stadium are daunting. Those privileged to stand close by a fence see what these courageous horses do. The top show jumper is a master of timing and balance and, don't forget, it is against the clock.

Close up and a study in concentration. The rider is Marcus Ehning. The German champion is compact and poised, with the hands of a maestro.

When things go wrong. Spencer Smith of the USA shows remarkable calm and sits tight when Belle D'Amour downs tools with alarming suddenness.

When it comes to horse shows, CHIO
Aachen is top of the league. The standard
is so high that falls are rare. When they
happen, the Stadium staff move in to
retrieve the horse and calm things down.

Vaulting

In 1997, when CHIO Aachen hosted the European Championships for the first time, vaulting appeared.

Like so many horse sports, vaulting has its origins as a cavalry discipline. The first European Championship was held in 1984. In vaulting, males and females are divided, which is unique in equestrian sport, but only for the individual medals. The six person team and the Pas de Deux can be all male, all female, or mixed.

The Albert-Vahle-Halle brings a theatrical atmosphere to the vaulting competition. It is perpetual motion. The test can last six minutes and the horse, guided by a sympathetic and skilled lunger, must canter throughout the performance. Vaulters wear colourful costumes and, as the song goes, fly through the air with the greatest of ease. Vaulting requires a ballerina's poise and harmony, total trust, split second timing, physical energy and courage.

Vaulting is a delight to see – it is Aachen beauty.

Joanne Eccles MBE,
World Vaulting Champion.

Vaulting was first recognised as an FEI discipline in 1983 and consists of an Individual, Pas de Deux and Team competitions.

Vaulting is often described as gymnastics on a horse. Then what is gymnastics? One internet definition is:

"Gymnastics is a type of sport that includes physical exercises requiring balance, strength, flexibility, agility, co-ordination, and endurance." We could rightly add courage, for in vaulting these physical exercises are accomplished on the back of a horse cantering in a 15 metre circle. Here a vaulter goes through her regime.

Youthful teams of 6 form up
and salute the judges. There
are variations on the salute, but
there is always a message of
smiling respect which seems to
say: "This is our chance and we
are going to enjoy it."

Elisabeth Simon elegant in black. She is the conductor. She controls the horse on the long lunge rein with minimum contact. She has to have a true feel for the horse and know all his ways. The vaulters rely on her horsemanship. She is a vital part of the team, vaulting is bound by a band of trust.

The art of the whip. A showjumper may have cause to deliver a sharp reminder, a jockey may reach for his whip in the final furlong, Indiana Jones may settle for a bullwhip crack, but the vaulting lunger's delicate flick of a whip is a piece of art.

To watch the vaulting championships at Aachen is to marvel, not only at the skill and daring of the vaulters, but the obedient patience and obliging willingness of the vaulting horse. He is a team member and his performance counts. His equipment must be of the best quality to withstand gymnastic feats by the vaulting teams. Of the 750 horses competing at CHIO, he is rather a special fellow.

'Parisian Pierrot, society's hero' wrote Noel Coward and here's another reminder that vaulting competitors, unlike dressage riders, can be offbeat and imaginative in their dress. This is vaulting World Cup gold medallist Janika Derks of Germany.

Five rows of pearls at a horse show? Surely not. But, in an echo of Audrey Hepburn in *Breakfast at Tiffany's*, here is perfect balance, glamour and high fashion chic.

Who could not be entranced by Kathrin Meyer?
Looking at her recalls the film director Billy Wilder,
when asked to explain the appeal of Audrey
Hepburn. Wilder said "Audrey was known for
something which I think has disappeared – that is
elegance, that is grace, and it's manners…" It has not
disappeared, the smiling Kathrin Meyer reassures us.
In 2023 Germany's vaulting star won the World Cup.

Choreography. Vaulting
aims for artistic impression,
for beauty. It appears to be
choreographed like a ballet.
Team Denmark creates
the vision of dance. In a
geometric threesome, the
squad shows how gesture and
movement combine to create
ballet beauty on horseback.

Golden Girl. She is almost flying – Team Koln-Donald from Germany.

Smiling through. It is a theatrical performance. A smile, as if to say 'look at me I'm having a wonderful time' is extra impressive when you are up aloft. This is the famous Team Neuss from Germany. The Pas de Deux is a dance duet when a couple performs the steps together. The vaulting equivalent on the back of a cantering horse is a remarkable sight.

Pauline Riedl of Germany
in 2019. Vaulting appeared
once, in the Olympic Games
of 1920, described as 'artistic
riding'. Pauline, a former World
Champion, proves the case.

Denmark's Sheena Bendixen
has a dancer's poise. She is a
picture of calm concentration
at the canter. She trusts her
lunger, her horse and herself.

Joanne Eccles, Great Britain.

Hannah Eccles, Great Britain.

Joanne Eccles and Hannah Eccles (GB) in 2014. The Eccles family, the sisters and their parents John and Jane, pioneered vaulting in the UK. In 2001 John Eccles set up Wee County Vaulters, a club for those seeking to take up the sport, at their farm in Scotland.

But the stars were his daughters who, with a horse called W.H. Bentley lunged by John himself, won a medal tally to dream about including a gold for Joanne at the World Equestrian Games (WEG) in 2014 and a bronze for the sisters in the Pas de Deux. Vaulting in Britain owes much to the Eccles family.

Lunger John Eccles with his daughters Joanne and Hannah.

Team Neuss, Germany

Watched by a discerning judge, Germany's Team Neuss reach the vaulting pinnacle with nonchalant ease. How high they go – what style.

The Austrian vaulters Millinger and Freund
show off beat style. At the the 2015 European
Championships this tiger/zebra duo brought a
touch of the wild. Costumes can be colourful,
individually creative, in contrast to the large
vaulting pad, usually white, and the plain
outfits, black or white, favoured by the lunger.

On my first visit to the Albert-Vahle-Halle, there were few Americans competing, but Mary McCormick was there. One of the most experienced and decorated vaulters in the United States, she was named Vaulter of the Year by the USEF in 2009 and 2011.

The German ace Jannis Drewell appears weightless in this high-flying leap, a study in athletic composure, in 2019. He won the World Cup in 2017 and defended his title in Dortmund in 2018.

Daniel Kaiser
of Germany.

Dominik Elder. The Austrian vaulter times his flying dismount like an Olympic high diver. Note the height attained.

In step. Everything is done in step. The Norka Squad team from Cologne look happy.

Lisa Wild. The Austrian leaves the arena at the European Championships 2015. Vaulting is a performance from start to finish. There is a drill which is respectfully followed when entering or leaving the hall, or saluting the judging panel. Here at the European Championships of 2015, Lisa Wild of Austria, known as 'the Backflip Queen' leaves the hall in perfect step.

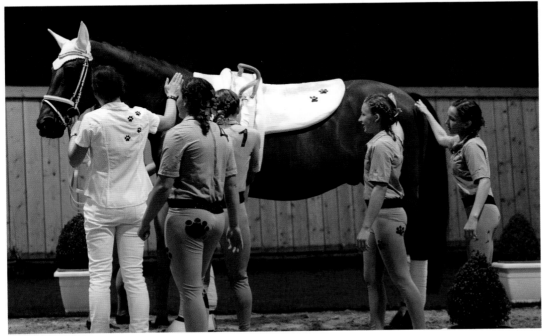

"Make much of your horses" is practised faithfully among vaulters. They show grateful thanks to their steady cantering friend with an outpouring of petting and patting.

The Swedish team and their connections wait anxiously, but not without relief, before entering the hall for the prize giving in 2011.

Vaulting is a sport for the young and team supporters show their colours at every opportunity.

German teams 1 and 2, first and second, enjoy their lap of honour to rapturous applause.

Never one to miss the action, Karli appears for the Sunday prize giving and to check up on his vaulting fan club. They are in very good heart and delighted to see him.

In a quiet corner, when all
is over, Vaulting Champion
Kristina Boe stands like a
ballerina as she is interviewed
by Dominique Wehrmann.

Horse and Symphony

The Horse and Symphony concert, performed on two gala evenings by the Sinfonieorchester Aachen, had its premiere at CHIO Aachen in 2002. The brochure says "magnificent music will meet up with magnificent equestrian sport." The concert is arranged under the supervision of Christopher Ward, General Music Director of Theatre Aachen and takes place in the floodlit Deutsche bank stadium. Here, Helen Langehanenberg, Grand Prix Dressage Aachen winner in 2012 and 2013 gives a display of elegance and beauty.

There is usually a theme. In 2018, it was "Mystical- fairytales, myths and heroes" so we had the music of Harry Potter, while the world class vaulters from Team Neuss performed to *Alice in Wonderland*, and the practically perfect in every way Mary Poppins dropped in to check on things.

In 2019, to honour France as partner country, the theme was "La vie est belle" and included a rousing version of the Can Can.

The Master of Ceremonies, Volker Raulf.

"Magnificent music will meet up with magnificent equestrian sport."

Let the drums roll out!
Let the trumpet call!
While the people shout
Strike up the band!

The Rodemis Band, in a tribute to America,
settled, not for Gershwin, but for John Philip
Sousa's Stars and Stripes for Ever. A quick
stepping march with fife and drum had the
Deutsche Bank stadium crowd toe tapping
to start the evening in soldierly style.

Show Programme

CHIO Aachen's Show Programme gives horse breeders a chance to appear in the finest show ring of all.

German horse breeding is highly successful, proved by the number of German bred horses who have won medals in the World Equestrian Games. The enthusiasm for horse sport and breeding can be measured by the amount of reading material on the subject. There is no other sport in Germany that can match the horse with regard to books and magazines.

Eventing

The Three Day Event, originally The Military and now called Eventing, was adopted at CHIO Aachen in 2007 following the success of the World Equestrian Games the year before. The cross-country course of 25 fences, is readily accessible for spectators, with the last fence in the stadium. The world's top riders compete.

The Three Day Event flourished in England due to the practical enthusiasm and generosity of two aristocrats, The Duke of Beaufort at Badminton, and The Marquess of Exeter (Olympic Gold Medal, 400 metres hurdles, 1928) at Burghley. Many eventing star riders are based in England and come to Aachen.

Sam Marsh, a legendary all round horseman and teacher, had a favourite quote: "There is no secret so close as that between a rider and his horse." A maxim for the Eventing rider, who must master dressage, cross-country and show jumping – on the same horse.

"There is no secret so close as that between a rider and his horse."

– Sam Marsh

A test for a super fit horse trained to gallop and jump over 25 fences across country against the clock and for a distance of 4 kilometres. This is Jonelle Price on Killbunny Andy in 2022

The Swedish international
Anna Freskgård sets out on the
cross country on her favourite
partner Box Qutie in 2018.

Ingrid Klimke's expression
appears to deny it, but her
style seems impeccable riding
FRH Butts Abraxos as she
clears the huge tree trunk that
forms the Rolex water jump.

Zara Phillips (now Mrs Mike Tindall) on Toytown listens intently in training for the 2007 event. If genes count, Zara is superbly qualified. She is the daughter of Captain Mark Phillips, who won Badminton four times, and HRH Princess Anne, European Champion at Burghley in 1971. She proved her heritage when she won the European Championship at Aachen in 2006.

Two Australian riders, Shane Rose and Isabel English, on the cross country course for the DHL Prize in 2017 show the exuberant power and spring of the event horse.

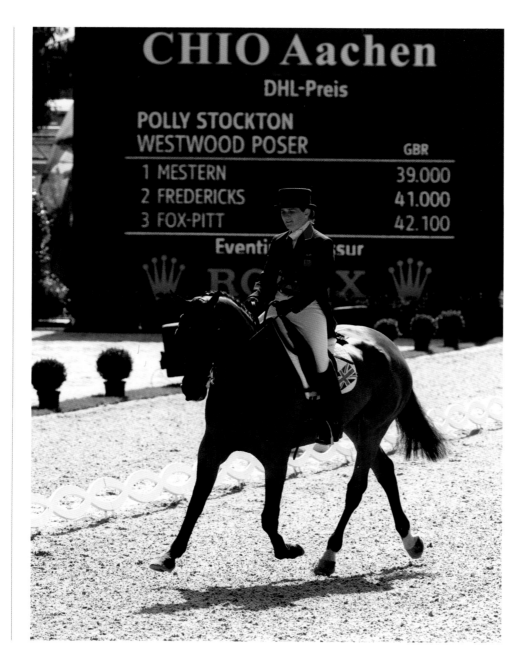

Polly Stockton (GB) on Westwood Poser in 2011. Polly had a long and distinguished career in top class eventing. She won the team gold at the 1994 European Young Rider Championships in 1994 and was the British National Champion in 1999. But the Burghley title eluded her. She was second in 2002, 2007 and 2009, a remarkable record.

Asked how she felt about Aachen, Polly replied: "For me, being chosen to represent team GB at Aachen was like being chosen for the Olympics. There is nothing that is comparable to Aachen, it is buzzing with equestrian super heroes and the atmosphere is indescribable."

Sara Algotsson Ostholt on Wega at
Aachen in 2011. The following year, again
riding Wega, she won the Individual
Silver Medal at the London Olympics.

William Coleman had early training with the US Olympic stars Karen and David O'Connor and aged 18 he won the gold medal at the North American Young Riders Championships. In 2012 he was picked for the US team at the London Olympics. In 2021. He won the SAP-Cup at Aachen riding Off The Record, the first American rider to do so.

Tim Price of New Zealand on Wesko in 2019. He won the German Championships in Luhmuhlen on this horse in 2014 and has competed in the Olympic Games in 2016 in Rio and the 2020 in Tokyo. He won bronze medals, individual and team in the World Championships in 2022.

He is married to Jonelle, a fellow New Zealand eventer, who won a team bronze at the London Olympics and was Badminton Champion in 2018. They live and train in England.

Mary King (GB) on Imperial Cavalier in 2011. She has a long and enviable record in the Three Day Event in England. Thousands of Pony Club girls, who dreamed one day to be like her, showed good judgement. She won the big ones, Badminton and Burghley and Lexington, and many medals beside. She competed in six Olympic Games in a career of sustained courageous riding talent spanning over twenty years. Her daughter Emily won the British Under 25 Championship in 2018. You might say 'it's all in the family'.

William Fox-Pitt's parents were tall and horsey. As the sport took off in England around 1960, you could not miss this eventing couple, Oliver Fox-Pitt and the fearless Marietta Speed. Both would ride at Badminton, but their son would reach the top and stay there for years.

William Fox-Pitt has many wins in a career which began 35 years ago. He has been champion at Burghley a record six times and competed in six Olympic Games. He appears to have won more medals and CCI ***** titles (14) than anyone else. It is a phenomenal achievement.

Michael Jung riding Halunke FBW in the dressage phase of the European Championships in 2015. On first watching this compact and brilliant rider, you feel at 5' 6" (1.7m) he is designed for the job. And yet he is cast against type, for today's champion eventers often appear lanky and long of limb. But Michael Jung seems to fit, at one with the horse, in dressage, cross-country and show jumping. His record proves it. He was the first rider hold the individual Olympic, World and European Championships at the same time.

La Biostheque Sam FBW is a name which does not easily trip off the tongue. Sam is easier. Experts said that he was not a natural talent, lacked quality, did not look the part. But he struck gold in the world of eventing and made Michael Jung a superstar. He was the first horse to hold all three major titles at the same time. That is the 2010 World Equestrian Games in Kentucky, the 2011 European Championships in Luhmulen and the 2012 Olympics in London. In 2015 he won at Burghley, adding the Badminton title the following year – "For me, the greatest." said Michael Jung.

Michael Jung, on his famous horse
fischerChipmunk FRH, shows the way in 2019.

The fence is beautifully built, but the sudden
circle of dark conifer must appear daunting to
horse and rider galloping against the clock.

Sandra Auffarth of Germany races home on her chestnut Opgun Louvo to win the 2014 DHL-Preis for Germany. The last fence is in the Main Stadium. Sandra Auffarth rides with dash, the cross country crowd responding with whistling, clapping and cheers. Her great partnership with Opgun Louvo began when she rode him as a 5-year-old. Together they won an individual bronze medal and team gold in the London Olympics. At the World Equestrian Games (WEG) in 2014 she was world champion to add to her Aachen success.

Nicola Wilson riding for Great Britain on her long time partner, Opposition Buzz. She was a member of the British team which won the DHL-Preis in 2011. An Olympic Silver Medallist and winner of the World Equestrian Games Team Gold, as well as the Individual European Championship and three European Team titles, she had a renowned career.

A terrible fall forced her retirement. Paralysed, she is determined to make a new start as a coach and mentor. Her bravery, her heroic will to win, to overcome every difficulty and her deep knowledge of the sport, will inspire riders everywhere.

Julia Krajewski won the DHL-Preis in 2018 riding Chipmunk FRH, but in Tokyo in 2020 she became the first lady rider to win the Individual Olympic Gold Medal for Eventing on Amande de B'Neviile, having won a Team silver in the Rio Games four years earlier.

In her FEI biography, she is asked for her sporting philosophy. She quoted Winston Churchill, a cadet destined for the cavalry, who passed out second in the Riding School at the Royal Military Academy Sandhurst:

"The trick is to get up one more time than you are knocked over."

There's something about a soldier... How good to see a rider in uniform, very right and proper. In the early days, the first half of the 20th Century, the Three Day Event was known as The Military. Only men took part, and in uniform. Women were barred. This is Fabrice Lucas on Nero du Jardin for the French Garde Republicaine entering the dressage arena in 2011.

Caroline Powell splashes through the water with total confidence in 2011. She rides the Irish horse Lenamore on which she won Burghley in 2010. The grey competed at Badminton seven times. The New Zealand rider moved to England to train and won a Team Bronze on Lenamore at the London Olympics in 2012. In 2024, at the age of 51, she proved her courage and her enduring riding spirit – she won Badminton on Greenacres Special Cavalier.

The beauty of timber. High on a hill, Clarke Johnstone (NZL) on Leopard's Action in 2022 tackles a log pile made by a master craftsman. The cross country fences at CHIO are beautifully designed, solid and yet with safety in mind for horse and rider should things go wrong.

Lauren Kieffer (now Lauren Nicholson) on Landmark's Monte Carlo for the USA in 2018. She began riding aged 6, but after high school, the gift of a Summer Camp with David and Karen O'Connor pointed the way. She took up a six year working student position with the O'Connors and in 2015 won a Team Gold at the Pan American Games on Meadowbrook's Scarlett.

The Great Triumvirate originally referred to Champion
Golfers, but when it comes to eventing Lucinda Fredericks
has conquered what might justifiably be called The Big Three
– the 4 Star Events at Badminton, Burghley and Lexington
on her mare Headley Britannia. A remarkable feat which she
achieved over the age of 40, after a long apprenticeship in the
sport. When she married Clayton Fredericks she represented
Australia and won a Silver Medal in the 2008 Olympic Games.
Here she competes on Flying Finish at CHIO in 2011.

Piggy French (now Mrs Tom March) on
Quarrycrest Echo at Chio in 2019. They won
a Team Gold at the World Equestrian Games
in 2018 and a Team Silver at the European
Championships the following year. In 2019
she won Badminton on Vanir Kamira. She
won Burghley in 2022, 21 years after her
first success in the European Young Riders
Championship. A great competitor.

Laura Collett on London 52 in 2019.
She began showing ponies, winning
the supreme pony title at The Horse
of the Year Show aged 13, but
eventing claimed her and she is a
British star. She won Badminton on
London 52 in 2022 and a Team Gold
in the Tokyo Olympic Games.

Another Irish horse who looks as though he is enjoying himself. With a name like Islandwood Captain Jack you sense that he is a superior person. He is ridden by Caroline Martin of the USA at CHIO in 2019, a study in concentration while bounding along, an eventing portrait.

Carriage Driving

Driving was a feature on the Soers show ground from the earliest days, but in 1930 came the supreme event, the Four-in-Hand. The first European Championships were held in 1971.

There are three tests: Dressage, Marathon and Obstacles (the Cones). You may prefer the dash and rough and tumble of the Marathon – HRH Prince Philip, a winning carriage driving competitor, referred to members of 'the Roll-Over Club' – but to see a sporting carriage and four pass through the cones, leaving them untouched, little more than an inch to spare either side, is beautiful.

The Marathon course is 17.5 kilometres long. There is a dress code. If a driver or passenger in the Marathon is found to be wearing shorts, a 10-point penalty is applied.

The Four-in-Hand competition requires great versatility, horsemanship and skill. Yet it brings an old world charm. It recalls the elegance of the horse age, which my grandfather told me he was glad he saw in London in 1898, the year Laurensberger Rennverein was founded in Aachen.

Every second counts.

Boyd Exell's name appears so many times on the CHIO winner's board that his rivals must feel they are up against 'the greatest'. In *Equestrian Life* magazine he was described as "Australian driving sensation". True indeed. If you look at the statistics on the FEI website, you will see that out of 192 starts Boyd Exell numbers 144 wins. Surely, in the business of horse sport, this is an astonishing record. Here he shows his mastery of Four-in-hand dressage. What a beautiful team.

Misdee Wrigley-Miller of the United States competing at CHIO in 2019. Her immaculate team glides along in the dressage phase, the driver dressed for Ascot. A serene scene and a contrast from the helter-skelter dash of the Marathon Cross-Country to come. Misdee Wrigley-Miller was in the United States team which won a Gold Medal at the World Equestrian Games at Tryon in 2018.

An attentive coachman, with a stern look, says "I don't want any nonsense from you" but this reminds us, in the push button age as we start the car and drive away, what is required to harness a coach and four. Bringing your team to compete at CHIO is a major task. Four horses and all that goes with them. We must thank the carriage drivers for their sporting endeavour and dedication. Their all-round driving skill is thrilling to watch, their presence a delight, their horses a wonder.

Chester Weber, a uniquely experienced American competition carriage driver devoted to Aachen, salutes the judges with a smile. He has competed at CHIO many times, winning in 2014, the year he was ranked FEI Top Four in Hand Driver He is immensely experienced and began young, competing in the World Pairs for the United States at the age of 18. In 2008 he was the first American to win an Individual Silver Medal in the Four-in-hand FEI World Driving Championships. Ten years later he won Team Gold in the World Equestrian Games at Tryon. Chester Weber is the most honoured carriage driver in the United States.

Karen Bassett is the most experienced British competition carriage driver. She began aged 8 and in 1995, at Saumur, she was the first lady ever to win an International Four-in-hand Carriage Driving competition.

In 1996 she won a bronze medal in the team event at the World Championships at Waregem. She took part in the European Championships at Aachen in 2015. The photograph emphasises the distance the driver, seated on the box, is from the leaders.

In 2015, the coffin of King Richard III (1452–1486), was mounted on a gun carriage drawn by a team of four horses and processed through Leicester for burial in the cathedral. The driver was Karen Bassett – an honour indeed.

Attention to detail in placing the cones in 2022. Delicacy is required, forefinger and thumb. Can it be true that a carriage and four, driven briskly, will inch between them leaving them in place? It is.

Georg von Stein of Germany at the Rolex water complex in 2019. He won a bronze medal in the Team Driving at the World Equestrian Games at Lexington in 2010. Here the impressive obstacle seems to eclipse the carriage.

IJsbrand Chardon uses all the aids in 2014 as he urges his team in a concentrated effort. One is vocal encouragement. The obstacles, the length of the carriage and team, the twists and turns needed for success are formidable. And, against the clock, it all has to be done at top speed, the driver's voice is invaluable. As the leaders swing out, you wonder how they will ever get round... and then suddenly they are through, off and away to shouts and wild applause.

The Marathon course asks many questions of horse and human, timing, accuracy, physical energy, stamina and concentration. It is inspiring to watch. Chester Weber judges the hairpin turn perfectly.

Boyd Exell in 2019. The Australian Supremo
has been World Champion six times and has
won the FEI World Cup Driving Championship
nine times. The photograph shows something
of the co-ordinated skill, the need to make
instant adjustments where centimetres count,
required of the Marathon Driver.

Thibault Coudry in at the deep end while competing for France in 2019. Generous horses excel as team members on the testing Marathon course. Their willingness to oblige and work together is a special feature of the Driving Class at CHIO, where horses join in harmony to win a medal. They are team players.

One four in hand driver, one eventer and one show jumper make up a team. Each must clear a number of varied obstacles, cones / marathon, cross country and show jumps. In a form of timed relay, the rider then climbs aboard the carriage which must complete the driving course. The fastest time wins, with each obstacle penalty adding 4 seconds. Here is show jumper Reed Kessler of the US partnered with Chester Weber.

Winners. Driving maestro Boyd Exell charges through the water as he competes in the Lavazza Cup in 2019. His passenger is another Aussie legend, eventer Andrew Hoy, who appears to be enjoying himself.

Andrew Hoy was 60 years old when he took part in this competition. In his great career he has won six Olympic Medals, three golds, two silvers and one bronze. He has won Burghley, Badminton and Kentucky. Here he storms through the water with an easy calm born of experience and love for the sport he has graced for so long.

Ros Canter (GB) shows her cross country mastery as she bounds through the water in the CHIO Cup in 2022. She won Team and Individual Gold at the World Equestrian Games in 2018. She is truly at the top. In 2023, she won the Badminton Horse Trials and the European Championship on Lordships Graffalo.

A parade and prize giving, means dressing up and the carriage drivers keep to tradition in the age of the open necked shirt. The Dutch wear orange, their colour of national unity – between yellow and red and seen easily at a distance, there could be no better colour for a grand horse show as Bram Chardon proves.

Germany's Mareike Harm was the first woman ever to compete in the Four-in-hand World Cup. She began with single horse carriage driving. In 2010 she became German Champion and Team World Champion. Then, in a leap of faith, she moved up to Four-in-hand demanding skill, accuracy, speed and considerable strength. In the Individual Combined Driving Competition she came 4th. There were 22 competitors.

Bram Chardon takes after his father, IJsbrand
Chardon, the Dutch legend who has won the
CHIO Driving Championship 13 times. He has
the privilege of learning from and competing
against his father. Here he takes part in the
procession of carriages on the final day in
2022. In the Individual he was placed 4th,
while his father came 2nd, going one better in
the Team competition, which father and son,
as best two to count, won for the Netherlands.

Ursula von der Leyen, President of the European Commission, a carriage is a fitting conveyance for such an eminent visitor. She is accompanied by Hermann Bühlbecker, owner Lambertz Group, sponsor and co-host of the Media Night.

The Vice-President of CHIO Baron Wolf von Buchholz with his wife, Baronin Amely von Buchholz.

Winners

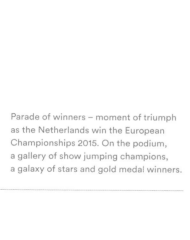

Parade of winners – moment of triumph
as the Netherlands win the European
Championships 2015. On the podium,
a gallery of show jumping champions,
a galaxy of stars and gold medal winners.

Collector's piece,
if not, it ought to be.
Rosettes celebrating
100 Years in 1998.

Hugo Simon leaves the arena on his great horse
E.T. after winning the Aachen Grand Prix in 1998,
the Centenary Year, at the age of 55. He was the
first person to win three World Cup titles and took
part in six Olympic Games, he became an Austrian
citizen in 1972. His love of show jumping endured.
He was still competing in 2011 at 68.

The Rolex Grand Slam Trophy is reverently borne into the Main Stadium for the Grand Prix of Aachen, which takes place on the last day, by two members of the Aachener Stadtreiter. The trophy was made by Garrard & Co, the famous jewellers and silversmiths established in London in 1735. The designer was Corinna Pike, heritage director at Garrard.

Janne Friederike Meyer won the Grand Prix of Aachen riding Cellagon Lambrasco in 2011. As the prize giving ceremony progressed, Cellagon thought he'd better get in on the act, or at least show his appreciation. He stood on his hind legs. Janne sat tight, the wave and the smile said: "I am on top of the world".

In 1955, Hans Günter Winkler riding Halla, won the World Jumping Championship at Aachen. This landmark win began a run of success for Herr Winkler, who remained loyal to CHIO to the extent of presenting The Halla Challenge Trophy in memory of his great mare. The trophy is presented to the most successful rider in six classical jumping competitions. Only one horse qualifies and the system means the rider with the most points wins.

Janne Friederike Meyer, the winner in 2011, poses for the photographers with Herr Winkler at right, together with Baron Wolf von Buchholz and her father, Friedrich Meyer, owner of Cellagon Lambrasco, who holds the Halla Trophy.

Waves and applause greet Germany's 2018 win in the Mercedes-Benz Nations Cup. In the centre standing is National Coach Otto Becker, who rode Cento to win the Grand Prix of Aachen in 2000.

Codex One, ridden by Christian Ahlmann for Germany, preserves a sense of occasion, almost a courtly bow, as he enters the Main Stadium to receive the Grand Prix of Aachen in 2014.

The Belgian rider Gregory Wathelet after
winning the Rolex Grand Prix on Coree in 2017.
The umbrellas are up as his lap of honour is
completed in a downpour. It is a matter of timing.
He won by 0.8 sec from Luciana Diniz on Fit for Fun.

Marcus Ehning not only won the Rolex Grand Prix in 2018 on Pret A Tout, but also the Halla Trophy for the most successful rider. He is seen here with owner Mrs Ruth Krech, Mrs Jytte Winkler and the Vice President Baron Wolf von Buchholz, who holds the Halla Trophy.

Gerrit Nieberg of Germany looks calm as he enters the Main Stadium in 2022. He is heading for the Rolex Grand Prix prize giving (€500,000 to the winner) in front of a capacity crowd of 40,000. The prize is his. The son of Lars, twice a Team Gold Medallist for Germany in the Olympic Games, his Grand Prix of Aachen win was the highlight of the 28-year-old rider's career.

The Press Conference on the last day after the Rolex Grand Prix in 2022. The winner Gerrit Nieberg tells of his triumph. Listening are: (l to r) Frank Rothenberger (Course Designer), Scott Brash (2nd), Nicola Philippaerts (3rd), Frank Kemperman (Show Director) and Dominique Wehrmann (Editor).

Kent Farrington of the United States answers a question in the press conference after his win on Gazelle in the Rolex Grand Prix of Aachen in 2019. Known as 'The Master of Faster', this was confirmed by the course designer Frank Rothenberger who said before the jump off that Kent Farrington is one of the fastest riders in the world. At left is Ben Maher (GB) who was third riding Explosion W.

Luciana Diniz of Portugal on Winningmood is presented with the Style Trophy in 2011 for the rider with the best style in the Rolex Grand Prix, the Grand Prix of Aachen, presented by Thomas de Maizière, Federal Minister of Defence.

Simone Blum of Germany followed her World Equestrian Games Individual Gold in 2018 by winning the Halla Challenge Trophy on DSP Alice in 2019. Awarded to the most successful show jumping rider in the classic competitions at CHIO, the prize, presented by Mrs Jytte Winkler, daughter of Hans Günter Winkler, the Halla is a perpetual challenge trophy and the winner receives a miniature in bronze. At the presentation are Mrs Winkler and Baron Wolf von Buchholz, Vice President of CHIO.

Elizabeth Madden of the United States receives the Stawag Prize on Breitling LS in 2017 from Dr Peter Asmuth, member of the executive board. Beezie Madden fulfilled the American Dream when she became the first woman to earn $1M in the sport of show jumping. A stalwart of the American team, she has won and won. Here a smiling handshake adds to her winning record.

Scott Brash holds the microphone on Hello Franklin after winning the Sparkasse Youngsters Cup Prize in 2019. The post match interview is a required skill for today's sports winners. Not much time to collect your thoughts, and a test of microphone skills when you speak, not in the club house, but from the back of a horse on its toes.

Thomas van Rijckevorsel (RSA)
wins on Lucy 781 FEI Youth
Equestrian Games 2022.
Lucy puts in a buck to celebrate,
while Thomas sits tight.

Penelope Leprevost won the Turkish Airlines Prize in 2015 on her famous chestnut mare Flora de Mariposa on which she won a Team Gold at Rio in 2016. She has her stand in for the prize giving well tied down but she is clearly enjoying herself.

Germany wins the Lambertz
Nations Cup in 2018. The victorious
team is greeted by a delighted
home crowd. The riders are (l to r)
Isabell Werth, Jessica von Bredow-
Werndl and Dorothee Schneider.

Thumbs up for Belgium,
winner of the Mercedes-
Benz Nations Prize in 2014.
The team consisted of Peter
Devos, Olivier Philippaerts, Los
Verlooy and Gregory Wathelet.

A sedate lap of honour for Alexander Matthias Rath and Totilas on their first appearance at CHIO in 2011. No triumphalism here. They won the Grand Prix and Totilas was still the World's No 1.

Victoria Max-Theurer wins the Preis der VUV, the Prix St Georges, on Augustin Old, in 2007. Thoughts of Vienna as the joyful Austrian rider waltzed around the arena.

Sönke Rothenberger on Cosmo 59 wins the
Lindt-Prize, The Grand Prix Special, in 2019
from his nearest rival Isabell Werth on Emilio, a
considerable feat for the 25-year-old rider German
born rider. Beginning in Pony Championships,
he has had Team Gold successes at European,
Olympic and World Championship level.

The 2012 Olympic Individual Gold medallist Valegro ridden by Charlotte Dujardin wins the Grand Prix of Aachen in 2014. Groom Alan Davies rewards the champion, a moment of relaxed calm after a barnstorming lap of honour.

Laura Graves on Verdades won the Meggle Prize,The FEI Grand Prix Special in 2017. This was the second individual qualifying competition for the Grand Prix Freestyle. The American rider bravely persevered with Verdades and was rewarded.

Another win. In 2018 Laura won the Preis der Familie Tesch, presented to her by Sabine Tesch.

The British Eventing Team: Nicola Wilson,
Mary King, William Fox-Pitt and Polly Stockton,
enjoy their success after winning the Team
competition for the DHL Prize in 2011. Michael
Jung of Germany won the Individual prize.

Julia Krajewski of Germany on Chipmunk FRH stand ready to receive the DHL Preis for Eventing as the top individual at CHIO in 2018. In 2020 she was the first lady rider to win the Individual Gold Medal at the Olympic Games in Tokyo.

Two tailored officials seem unconcerned as Jessica Kurten of Ireland on Quibell gallops by on her lap of honour. She has just won the AachenMünchener Prize, a jumping competition for horses not competing in the Rolex Grand Prix.

"And as fancy grows prophetic
I anticipate the hour,
When I soar by feats athletic
To the shining ranks of power."

What a great idea to display the names of
those who have soared by feats athletic
for all to admire.

With his name on the top of the leader board at Badminton on May 12th 2024, there were many willing William Fox-Pitt to win. But this artful exponent of clear rounds found himself denied. Without hesitation he announced his retirement from Badminton the glorious Three Day Event he had adorned in a career spanning 35 years. His record is astonishing, his courage indomitable. He will be missed all over the Equestrian World. At CHIO Aachen he won a Team Gold in 2011.

Exuberant delight from IJsbrand Chardon
as he records another win at CHIO in a
2018 triumph for the Netherlands, winners
of the Team Driving Nations Cup for
Combined Driving as well as the The Prize
of the Richard Talbot Family, Aachen.

Two vaulting champions in 2017 and 2019 – Germany's Janika Derks and Thomas Brusewitz.

Germany's triumph and one
for the family album – today,
who needs photographers?

The Silver Camera Award 2010/2011. The finalists face the camera, something that the great Frenchman Henri Cartier-Bresson said photographers should never do. The winner is Julia Rau from Mainz. The runners up are Reuters photo journalist Caren Firouz and the well known Dutch equestrian photographer Arnd Bronkhorst. The Silver Camera Award attracts over 100 entries and goes to the photographer who has taken the best equestrian sport photo over the last twelve months. A hard task to judge.

Julia Rau, tall and athletic, was always on the move. Armed with what looked to be a fast 200 mm lens attached to a single stick 'monopod', she raced around Soers in pursuit of pictures. She was rewarded. Her vaulting photograph won The Silver Camera. Congratulations!

233

Fashion

Kristina Bröring-Sprehe and the SOXX range she endorses. Many riders have been glad to put their names to equestrian products and fashion clothing ranges.

Kristina Sprehe

Team - Silbermedaillengewinnerin Dressur
Olympische Spiele 2012

Julia Mestern shows an ineffable
style, based on attention to detail,
which extends to the immaculate
plaiting of her horse, dressage chic.

A designer look for 2015, the year of the European Championships. Distinctive magenta was chosen for the arena prize giving assistants and the effect was charming.

The care with which this stylish photographer lines up her shot is clear to see. Is she waiting for Cartier-Bresson's 'decisive moment'?

"Blue jeans are the most beautiful thing since the gondola" said *Vogue* editor Diana Vreeland and you see a lot of blue jeans in the horsey world. The Russian photographer Natalia Kostikova, about to photograph the carriage driving in 2015, settled for denim.

A delight at CHIO is the efficiency and courtesy of the attendant staff, there are no other words for them, this is elegance in attendance. Looking the part is Delia Marcelli, the perfect hostess.

French luxury design, but how right it is that Hermes should show its master saddler at work. Although you may think of silk scarves, the Company began as makers of harness in Paris in 1837. The Hermes business was founded on craftsmanship in leather for the horse trade.

Brown boots appear in the practice arenas at Aachen and sometimes in the arena. Meredith Michaels-Beerbaum wore them at CHIO on her last winning appearance on Shutterfly. This laced masterpiece could not be missed.

The primary colours of red and blue look right in the Aachen show jumping arena. Lucy Davis wears the red of the United States and a beautiful coat, too. Luciana Diniz of Portugal settles for blue.

The Austrian rider, Victoria Max-Theurer, a winner at CHIO, chooses a brown tailcoat, with a distinctive stripe, and top hat to match, a stylish choice – a welcome change from funereal black, a dress code bound by tradition.

Riding breeches were once baggy, an almost butterfly shape. Not now. This is the new look: skin tight breeches, high boots with some gem adornment, and a neat custom tailored coat which could have begun life in Coco Chanel's atelier.

When it comes to an elegant look, the top hat beats the protective helmet, but not for safety. Laura Graves aims to stay safe in a perfectly fitted hat. Gold buttons with the five Olympic rings set off her immaculate coat, in what used to be called 'midnight blue.'

Denise Nekeman the high point of equestrian cool in 2017. Some say women look their best in riding clothes, or was it hunting clothes? Here is the off duty look of the International Dressage rider at CHIO.

It's the European Championships and they support Sweden. No doubt they ride beautifully. Unaware, they bring to the CHIO scene a brand of youthful glamour and natural style.

Evening light, lengthening shadows, the magic hour... it's time for cocktail parties and receptions on the last day, and another fashion style.

Old Glory, the nickname for the flag of the United States, finds a new role. No doubt who these two are supporting. The stars and stripes are always in fashion.

More red white and blue. Karen Bassett of Great Britain, patriotic and formal in the European Championships 2015.

Sir Alfred Munnings painted women riding
sidesaddle often. His 1930s picture "Why Weren't
You Out Yesterday?" shows three ladies at a meet
of hounds. The central figure is riding a grey.

Amy Bryan-Dowell rides a grey in the Main Stadium
for a display by the Side Saddle Association in 2015.
Her black habit with lapels cut to reveal her white
waistcoat and stock with top hat are as worn by the
ladies in the painting. A Munnings model indeed.

The film director Alfred Hitchcock was
known for his casting. The 'Hitchcock
blonde', a cool beauty, was readily
recognised for class, style and ladylike
qualities. This vaulting star, with her
floaty dress, her high fashion style, would
no doubt have caught the director's eye.

Management

Attention to detail is the hallmark of CHIO Aachen's management. Here we see proof of the "seeing eye" in action as Jana Kun, Discipline Manager Dressage, emphasises a point to Show Director Frank Kemperman in 2015, with Rob de Bruin, Technical Delegate (Vaulting), looking on.

Approximately 1300 dedicated staff and volunteers return to Soers for duty year after year to guarantee that CHIO Aachen keeps its high standards.

The International Federation for Equestrian Sports, with its headquarters in Lausanne, founded in 1921, is the international Governing body of equestrian sports. An FEI Code of Conduct safeguards the welfare of horses from physical abuse or doping. This is FEI Steward Joelle Beier-Kinnen at the FEI European Championships in 2015.

Famous CHIO Steward Hubert Coonen retires after 40 years service. Unmistakable and always at the entry to the stadium, everyone knows him. The support of people like Hubert, the courteous handling of spectators, makes a visit to CHIO doubly enjoyable.

A voice said: "Could you take a picture? "I nervously said "yes". "We'd like one of the Dressage Jury." A quick snap was all I could manage.

Here (l to r) in 2018 are: Juan Carlos Campos Escribano, Hans Christian Matthiesen, Susan Hoevenaars, Ulrike Nivelle and Christof Umbach.

It is well to remember the vital part judges play. What the lawyers call due diligence is required. They must not miss a thing. It is an exercise in concentration, in technical expertise and unbiased judgement.

Custom transport, and a steady hand, is required to deliver an essential ingredient of The Warsteiner Prize. It goes to Meredith Michaels-Beerbaum who has just won the prize on Shutterfly in 2011.

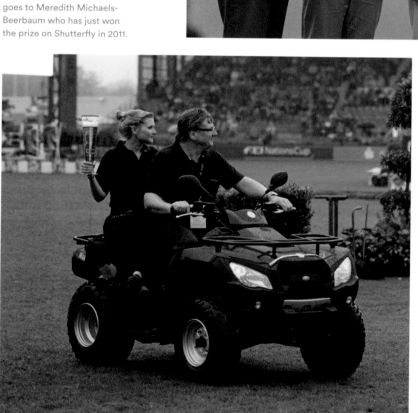

The management is wunderschönen – beautiful. Consider these two prize-giving assistants. They are flawlessly dressed. A Madison Avenue fashion stylist would not do better. And they walk together in perfect step. They do not wander about. In the slap-happy world of today, a world where it seems anything goes, CHIO Aachen respects tradition and high standards.

The show jumps at Aachan are beautifully made, colourful and imaginative. The physical energy required to build the courses (and alter them for jump offs) during the week of competition is another aspect of CHIO one takes for granted. That well-known feature, the Aachen Globe, is carefully handled by the DHL team.

The summer sun dries the surface in the Deutsche Bank Stadium. A water bowser keeps the surface as it should be.

DHL sponsors the arena party and it is hard work on the Mercedes-Benz Nations Cup evening. Eight Teams and two rounds. They are not always impartial. Hence their delight in Germany's 2018 victory.

Spectators waiting to register for Media
Night in 2015. The handling of spectators,
there are 450.000 visitors, requires
efficiency, teamwork and courtesy.

On the first Sunday, an Ecumenical Church Service is held in the Deutsche Bank Stadium. As you would expect, horses take part. After the service, appropriately, the officiating clergy leave the Stadium in a horse drawn carriage.

In the foyer of the Champions' Circle, you may see a distinguished gentleman, in a custom tailored suit and panama hat, seated at the piano. He is Bob Chisholm, who has been entertaining guests for over twenty years. He says "'All who come to the Soers will feel good." He loves CHIO Aachen, describing it as "every year the high point on my calendar." Here he takes a break in his inimitable style. Thank you, Bob, friend of CHIO.

Lunch in The Riders Club and a chance to meet in a most hospitable atmosphere. Competitors and the media are generously treated and the food and service are excellent. Another aspect of management which runs smoothly and enjoyably.

Among the photographers at CHIO, Arnd Bronkhurst is a man apart. There is his great height, his energy, his long experience, his personality, his talent. For 25 years he has travelled the world and his archive shows horse photography at its finest. As the official photographer to CHIO Aachen, he is sometimes in charge of the roaming photo pack, but not this time. He stands alone in the arena, alert and concentrating, a mobile call no doubt confirming his next assignment. Note his equipment, a heavy burden, but he can cover everything.

Isabell Werth won the Grand Prix on Bella Rose on 21st July 2019, her 50th birthday, to universal acclaim and birthday red roses.

The media move in after her win, intent on 'the story behind the story', the birthday, what's next? The star is a model of composure, an old hand when it comes to sound bites.

The Stars

The forecourt, outside the offices of Aachen-Laurensberger Rennverein e.V., recalls Grauman's Chinese Theatre, and the stars of Hollywood, whose foot and hand prints are imprinted. Here are the shoes of star horses.

"Star? Of course, I'm a star! I say hello to everyone and they all remember ME!" says Karli.

John Whitaker at CHIO in 1998. 24 years later at 66, he was again at Aachen, in the British team for the Nations Cup. He is the eldest of the Whitaker family from Yorkshire who founded a show jumping dynasty. He has competed in 39 major international championships winning 24 medals.

Dr Reiner Klimke studies a photograph at CHIO in 1998. He combined his work as a full-time lawyer with outstanding success as an international dressage rider and teacher. On his horse Ahlerich, trained by his wife Ruth, he brought classical dressage to the world, notably in the 1984 Olympic Games when, at the age of 48, he won the Individual Gold Medal. He won the Grand Prix of Aachen 8 times. His death, at 63, was a shattering loss. He was admitted to the Hall of Fame of German Sports.

At Goodwood, England, in 1978, for the Dressage World Championships, you could watch the stars riding in. One man, hatless and riding a chestnut, stood out. He made it look easy. He seemed way ahead of the rest. An enquiry revealed his name: "Oh, that's Harry Boldt." No wonder. The nonchalant ease and effectiveness of Harry Boldt's riding is a lasting memory.

Harry Boldt won many medals and was awarded the Silver Bay Leaf, the highest German Sports Award. He was chief coach to the West German Dressage team and wrote an important textbook, *Das DressurPferd* (The Dressage Horse). Here, nearing 90, he reflects on the CHIO scene.

The daughter of Reiner and Ruth Klimke, Ingrid is a star event rider. She won a Team Gold Medal at the 2008 and 2012 Olympic Games. In 2012, she was appointed Reitmeister, an honoured title awarded by the German Equestrian Federation. Slim and super fit, she is a remarkable riding talent. In 2022 she joined the German Dressage team at the World Championships and won a bronze medal.

Anky van Grunsven, the triple individual Olympic Dressage Gold Medallist, showed her athleticism, versatility and balance at speed, when the European Reining Championships were held at Aachen in 2015. Spectators, more accustomed to the serene calm of her piaffe, marvelled at her dashing display, her consummate skill. She literally changed horses and there she was, 'underneath the Western skies.'

Madeleine Winter-Schulze surely ranks as a star for her generous support of riders and her delight in the ownership of beautiful horses. She has decided to retire one of her stars. Here she is outside Bella Rose's stable on the day in 2022 when the mare's retirement was announced.

Bella Rose passes by on her final lap of honour. Isabell Werth rides Madeleine Winter-Schulze's champion mare into the dressage history books, the hall of fame.

Dressage rider Steffen Peters gained his US Citizenship in 1992. He said: "The whole idea of being so patriotic, of feeling so close to one's country makes a difference. There are not too many other countries where the people are so patriotic. I really enjoy this about America." Steffen Peters has competed in five Olympic Games. Aspiration and hard work.
The American Dream.

Lisa Wilcox returned to her homeland America with a deep knowledge of classical dressage and how to ride and train horses after years working in Europe. She is bringing on horses and teaching with top prizes in her sights. She holds an Olympic Team bronze and a World Championship Team Silver. Always immaculate, it was no surprise she was chosen to model riding clothes. She is a star.

Laura Graves first wanted to represent the US in Eventing, but switched to dressage. She went to the top on her famous horse Verdades, which she had as a foal when she was 15, breaking him in herself. Laura described him as a horse of a lifetime. They were a 'visual partnership' at Aachen, the tall, slim American on a sturdy supercharged horse. Their relationship? Close. They really knew each other. And it was always good to watch.

Two Gold Medals and you and your horse become the focus of all eyes. But sometimes, you can escape the pressure of celebrity status for a quiet moment and time to think. Here's Charlotte Dujardin relaxing with Valegro, her champion, far from the crowd.

Seeing Charlotte Fry aged 23 at Aachen you are struck by her youth and her concentration. When all is over she resets to a wide smile. The relief after the pent up feeling, the tethered excitement, before a dressage test must be blissful. Lottie Fry left home to train in Denmark. Her pursuit of excellence paid off. At 26 she was World Champion.

Kristina Bröring-Sprehe on her Premium Hanoverian stallion Desperados, winner of many medals including the Grand Prix of Aachen. Kristina and Desperados won team gold and Grand Prix Special silver at the 2014 World Equestrian Games and team and Grand Prix Special bronze and Kur Silver at the 2015 European Championships at Aachen, before winning team gold and individual bronze at the Rio Olympic Games in 2016. Desperados was much sought after in the quest to breed dressage champions.

Carl Hester has had a stellar career in dressage. His influence on the sport in England is profound as a teacher and competitor. In 1992 he was the youngest British rider ever to appear in the Olympic Games. His inspired ownership of Valegro, leading to Charlotte Dujardin's double Gold Medal success, ensured his place in British dressage history.

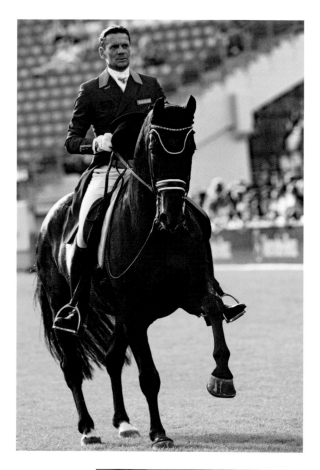

Edward Gal's name is forever linked with Totilas, the black stallion who became the most famous dressage horse in the world. Together they were triple gold medallists at the 2010 FEI World Games, the first dressage partnership to achieve this scintillating clean sweep. The sale of Totilas rocked the dressage world. There was much talk of the horse – but what about the rider who had created his magic? Edward Gal went on to confirm his talent with Glock's Undercover.

Nadine Capellmann has competed at 4 European Championships, 3 World Equestrian Games and the Olympics at Sydney and Beijing. She won the Grand Prix of Aachen in 2002 with Farbenfroh and in 2006 with Elvis VA, her ride in 2007.

At the age of 17 Victoria Max-Theurer was the youngest rider to take part in the European Dressage Championship in 2003. In 2007 she rode the stallion Augustin to win the Prix St Georges at Aachen. A long-standing Austrian team member, here she takes hold after an unexpected 'spook' while leaving the arena.

Dutch dressage champion Adelinde Cornelissen achieved great success with her chestnut Jerich Parzival. She won one World Championship, four European Championships and two World Cup gold medals. At the London Olympic Games she won the individual silver medal.

Cathrine Dufour of Denmark on Vamos Amigos won the Grand Prix of Aachen, awarded on a points system, she has restored Denmark to the top league in world dressage. She has everything to play for.

Beatriz Ferrer-Salat competing in 2011. She has represented Spain in the Atlanta, Barcelona, Sydney, Athens, Rio and Tokyo Olympics, a remarkable achievement. There is something regal about her, an immaculate old style elegance. She is another brave rider. A serious riding accident in 2020 forced her to lay off for 18 months. She came back to become Spanish National Champion for the 10th time.

Jessica von Bredow-Werndl is generally smiling. But in this 2015 photograph she is all business, focussed intently on the job in hand. She loves horses and says "For me it is all about the love for the horse". Her horses have brought her stardom. She is a multiple German Champion, European and World Team Champion and Olympic Team and Individual Gold Medallist.

Marcus Ehning on Funky Fred for Germany in the 2019 Nations Cup. He has been called 'the maestro' and with good reason. He has won the Rolex Grand Prix at Aachen three times and many more titles besides. He is a model rider of quiet style. When he wins there is no triumphalism. He is an admirer of John Whitaker. He is a master of the show jumping scene.

Helen Langehanenberg won the Grand Prix of Aachen in 2012 and again in 2013 riding Damon Hill. She was a member of the German silver medal winning team at the London Olympics in 2012. What a pleasure it was to see her give a beautiful display amid the dramatic theatre lights of Horse & Symphony. Glamorous dancing dressage.

Meredith Michaels-Beerbaum has the microphone but is overcome before paying tribute to her favourite show jumping star Shutterfly on his retirement in 2011. Shutterfly seems to be taking his last bow. Meredith Michaels-Beerbaum came to Germany from the United States. She was the first woman show jumper to be ranked World No 1 and the first woman to win the World Cup three times. Shutterfly was difficult, but she persevered. He became a legend, winning, among many other titles, The Grand Prix at Aachen in 2005.

Reviewing his career in an interview for the *CHIO Aachen* magazine, Ludger Beerbaum said that his double gold on Ratina at the European Championships in Mannheim in 1997 was a highlight. He had won the Grand Prix of Aachen the previous year and an Olympic Team Gold medal. He spoke of the unparalleled atmosphere and enthusiasm of the spectators at CHIO Aachen. Here he rides Madeleine Winter-Schulze's Couleur Rubin in 2011.

It is remarkable how show jumpers retain their eye for a fence, their timing, their speed, their balance and above all their nerve over the years, and in Beezie Madden's case decades. She began riding Grand Prix at the age of 22 in 1985. She won the Grand Prix of Aachen on Authentic in 2007 In 2014 riding Cortes C she was the first woman to win the King George V Gold Cup at Hickstead, then she won the cup again, 'back to back'. She won the Longines World Cup twice, in 2018, at 54, the oldest athlete to do so. After 35 years at top level she decided to 'semi-retire'.

A show jumping wonder.

Laura Kraut on Cedric in the Nations Cup 2011, the horse that won her a team Gold Medal at the Beijing 2008 Olympics. Appearing regularly at CHIO Aachen, she has been at the top for decades. In 2022, she was named International Equestrian of the Year by the United States Equestrian Federation. Her record of dedication in training horses, her endurance, her charitable work and sponsorships, together with her many successes, reflect the benefits of a full career in the sport.

Kent Farrington on Willow in the Mercedes-Benz Nations Cup in 2014. He started his own business at 21 and became one of the fastest riders to earn $1M in prize money. He had worked his way up from learning to ride on carriage horses as a boy in Chicago. He made No 1 in the World rankings and looks the part in every way, proved by his two electric clear rounds to win the Rolex Grand Prix on Gazelle in 2019.

A veteran of five Olympic Games, McLain Ward cites winning the Individual Gold on HH Azur at the World Cup in Omaha in 2017 as the highlight of his career. The photograph shows him driving hard in a jump off at speed. Total concentration, strength, balance, co-ordination of eye, hand and leg, to beat the clock.

Penelope Leprevost, a regular competitor at Aachen, allows herself a break. Her cool pose recalls film stars of old when cigarettes added to on screen allure. She is a great competitor for France. Riding Flora de Mariposa, she was a member of the team that won Gold at the Rio Olympic Games in 2016. Flying round, she adds panache to the Aachen ring.

Christian Ahlmann has just won the Rolex Grand Prix on Codex One in 2014. He started young, at the European Championships in 1989 at the age of 15. In 2003, he became European Champion on Coster. In December 2012 he was ranked No 1 in the world.

Daniel Deusser on Killer Queen Vdm won the Rolex Grand Prix of Aachen in 2021. The tall German has been highly successful since he first appeared in the European Young Rider Championships in 2002, and that is twenty-one years ago. In 2014 he won individual Gold in the World Cup Final on Cornet d'Amour.

Anne Kursinski showing the determination that has carried her to five Olympic Games and The Grand Prix of Aachen on Starman in 1991. In that year, the US Olympic Committee voted her Female Equestrian Athlete of the Year and in 2017 she was inducted into the Show Jumping Hall of Fame. A member of 47 US Nations Cup Teams, she describes herself as a Riding and Jumping Mentor and is in much demand as a trainer and teacher.

Luciana Diniz riding Fit for Fun in the Rolex Grand Prix 2017. Her two clear rounds led to an agonising jump off with Gregory Wathelet. She lost by less than a second. In 2015 she won the Longines Champions Tour. Born in Brazil, she began by winning Junior and Children's Jumping Championships. Apart from riding, she has developed an "informal education philosophy" known as G.R.O.W. to teach adults and children.

Nights of gladness, or sometimes tears, The Mercedes-Benz Nations Cup on the Thursday at CHIO. The main stadium is floodlit and that brings the contrast of theatre lighting which adds to the exciting atmosphere. It gives us a profile portrait of Steve Guerdat, the 2012 Olympic Individual Gold Medallist, riding Hannah in the 2018 Nations Cup.

Double Olympic Gold Medal winner (Individual and Team) Ben Maher has represented Britain in four Olympic Games. He started on winning form when he won the Hickstead Derby in 2005 and has been in the money ever since. Here he rides his Olympic horse, the commanding chestnut Explosion W, in the Rolex Grand Prix in 2019. He was third. But that was still good enough for him to take home a prize of €150,000.

Gregory Wathelet, completing his round in the European Jumping Championships held at Aachen in 2015, riding Conrad de Hus. He was second in The Rolex European Championships and again second in the FEI Overall Individual Championships. Gregory Wathelet was rewarded when he won the Rolex Grand Prix of Aachen in 2017. He was a member of the Belgian team which won the Nations Cup in 2014.

Scott Brash (GB) is the only rider to have won the Rolex Grand Slam of Show Jumping, a remarkable feat. At Spruce Meadows in Canada, against intense competition, the Scottish rider jumped clear in both rounds for his third victory in a row after Geneva and Aachen. The horse was Hello Sanctos, the date was 13th September 2015. Thanks to the generosity of Rolex, the reward, you might say, was "beyond the dreams of avarice." Scott Brash earned a bonus of 1 million euros to add to his already substantial prize-money. Congratulations!

'More stars than there are in heaven'
claimed Metro-Goldwyn-Mayer
and the same could be said for New
Zealand when it comes to eventing.
Blyth Tait, Mark Todd, Clarke
Johnstone and Tim Price are a fine
galaxy. Here they celebrate winning
the DHL Prize in 2018.

It's hats off for IJsbrand Chardon as he celebrates
his 2018 win in the Combined Driving Competition.
His style and timing have brought him many victories
and the crowd applauds his lap of honour. He has
dominated the sport of carriage driving for three
decades, winning his first World Championship in
1988. In 2002 he won team and individual World
championships medals at Jerez. He has won the
Championship at CHIO Aachen 13 times.

With his first win at the age of 16, Australia's Boyd Exell set out on a career which led to 6 World Championships and 10 World Cup Driving titles. For his services to equestrian sport he was awarded the Order of Australia. He says he can feel the horses down the rein, how they feel. What a huge advantage for a carriage driver. Boyd Exell's connection with his horses, his remarkable accord has made him the man to beat.

A dedicated driver from the USA who competes regularly at CHIO Aachen, bringing his young family over to support him. He has been massively successful. One of his memorable moments was to win the championship at the Royal Windsor Horse Show two years running and receive congratulations from Her Majesty The Queen. Chester Weber is an important figure in the world of carriage driving which he has done so much to promote in the United States and throughout the world.

Closing Ceremony

Leading dressage riders show their paces in the Main Stadium as part of the Closing Ceremony.

Stewards wait to open the gates to begin the Closing Ceremony.

The late afternoon scene. The circular building is the Judges' Tower from which there is an unrivalled view.

278

Goodbye until next year. Carriage horses enjoy themselves amid the expanse of the Main Stadium Arena. This is Ferenc Jr. Galbács of Hungary with his team.

The competitors circle the arena waving their handkerchiefs to the rousing tones of the German folk song 'Muss i denn zum Stadtele hinaus' which is played over and over again. The spectators wave back. There is a party atmosphere known as 'The Aachen Wave.'

For once the cheerful Karli
is not his usual happy self.
He waves forlornly, but he
looks forward to next year
when he will be back to
welcome everyone again.

German pop star Max
Giesinger amid a barrage
of fireworks brings CHIO
Aachen 2022 to a close.
Everyone "gets with the beat."

Farewell to Frank

At the heart of affairs is Chio Aachen Show Director, Frank Kemperman. To see him at work is a lesson in management. He leads from the front. He is everywhere, helping his 1,300 staff / volunteers achieve the perfection for which CHIO Aachen is famous.

He was always on the move, but ready to take a call and listen. He saw that everyone is looked after. As he led a press tour of the stables, his love of horses became obvious. He said the stables were his favourite place: "This is where I started".

Fluttering hankies and cheers from spectators and competitors in the vast arena greet the Chairman of the Board, Frank Kemperman. He is driven round the Stadium in a charming tribute to mark the legendary Dutchman's retirement after 29 years in 2022. The colour is orange – a nice touch. Frank Kemperman was appointed Knight of the Order of Orange Nassau by Queen Beatrix for his work during the FEI World Equestrian Games Aachen 2006.

After all the ceremony, razzmatazz and well-wishing goodbyes, I picked up my gear to go back to my hotel. I walked out through the deserted Office Reception. Then, I saw a gentleman all by himself playing with what I took to be his grandchild. It was Frank Kemperman. I thought what a sweet picture and walked on.

Acknowledgements

Thank you to the many people who helped make this book possible.

First, my grateful thanks to Isabell Werth for so kindly writing the foreword.

I am most grateful to Minnie Churchill for her enthusiasm for the book and, at just the right time, for putting me on the right path.

My sincere thanks to Niels Knippertz, Melanie Psychny, Alina Gotzeiner, Carl Hester, Saskia Stahl-Farrell, Claire Oliver, John Richards, Marc Lorenz of Photo Preim Aachen, Marcel Koepper, Magnus Caspar, Will Lee, Ciaran Campbell, Polly Stockton, Camilla Case, John, Joanne and Hannah Eccles for their help.

Jan Westmark Bauer, Editor of *Sidelines* magazine in the United States, was a huge support throughout my many visits to CHIO. Thank you.

My thanks to Edith de Reys and the CHIO Press Centre, the photo co-ordinators and show ground stewards for their kindliness and efficiency, not forgetting the hospitality in the Riders Club.

My thanks to the management of ALRV, to the competitors and their horses for the glorious show they create, not forgetting my respected and congenial fellow – photographers.

I would like to thank my publishers Lord Strathcarron and Ryan Gearing of the Unicorn Publishing Group for agreeing to go ahead, for their advice and their care and attention to detail in design and production.

My only sadness is that my dear friend, the late Ed Burrows, a fervent supporter of the project from the very beginning, whose judgment I valued so highly, did not live to see this book.

Lastly, my wife Anne. I thank her for her support during what for me was a period of solitary confinement, which she endured while encouraging me throughout – and with good advice, too.

Published in 2024 by Unicorn an imprint of
Unicorn Publishing Group
Charleston Studio
Meadow Business Centre
Lewes BN8 5RW
www.unicornpublishing.org

Text and photographs © John Monoprio

ISBN 978-1-911397-98-4

10 9 8 7 6 5 4 3 2 1

Designed by Matthew Wilson
Printed by Fine Tone Ltd

Front cover: Meredith Michaels-Beerbaum on Fibonacci.
Back cover: Laura Graves on Verdades.